# LANGUAGE ARTS

# WEEKLY

# PRACTICE

## Grade 4

Credits
Authors: Mitchell Cooper, Margie Glickman Jones, Lisa McFarren
Copy Editor: Christine Schwab

Visit *carsondellosa.com* for correlations to Common Core, state, national, and Canadian provincial standards.

Carson-Dellosa Publishing, LLC
PO Box 35665
Greensboro, NC 27425 USA
carsondellosa.com

978-1-4838-2792-6
01-053167784

# Table of Contents

# Introduction

The Weekly Practice series provides 40 weeks of essential daily practice in either math or language arts. It is the perfect supplement to any classroom curriculum and provides standards-based activities for every day of the week but Friday.

The activities are intended as homework assignments for Monday through Thursday and cover a wide spectrum of standards-based skills. The skills are presented at random to provide comprehensive learning but are repeated systematically throughout the book. The intention is to offer regular, focused practice to ensure mastery and retention.

Each 192-page book provides 40 weeks of reproducible pages, a standards alignment matrix, flash cards, and an answer key. The reproducible pages are perfect for homework but also work well for morning work, early finishers, and warm-up activities.

# About This Book

Each page contains a variety of short, fun exercises that build in difficulty across the span of the book. The activities are divided into two sections:

- The Daily Extension Activities at the front of the book are intended to engage both student and family. These off-the-page activities are simple and fun so that students will look forward to this practice time at home. The activities span one week at a time. The instructions are clear and simple so that students can follow them with or without assistance in their homes. None need be returned to school.

- The daily practice section involves more comprehensive learning. Because of the simplicity of directions and straightforward tasks, students will be able to complete most tasks independently in a short period of time. There are four pages of activities per week, allowing for testing or a student break on Friday if desired. These pages are intended to be brought back to school.

Pages can be offered in any order, making it possible to reinforce specific skills when needed. However, skills are repeated regularly throughout the book to ensure retention over time, making a strong case for using pages sequentially.

An answer key is included for the daily practice section. You can check answers as a group for a quick follow-up lesson or monitor students' progress individually. Follow the basic page layout provided at the beginning of the answer key to match answers to page placement. Also included in the book is a set of flash cards. Reproduce them to give to students for at-home practice, or place them in classroom centers.

# Common Core State Standards
## Alignment Matrix

| Standards | W1 | W2 | W3 | W4 | W5 | W6 | W7 | W8 | W9 | W10 | W11 | W12 | W13 | W14 | W15 | W16 | W17 | W18 | W19 | W20 |
|---|---|---|---|---|---|---|---|---|---|---|---|---|---|---|---|---|---|---|---|---|
| 4.RL.1 |  |  |  |  |  |  |  |  | • |  | • |  |  |  |  |  | • |  |  |  |
| 4.RL.2 |  | • |  |  |  | • |  |  | • |  |  |  |  |  |  |  |  |  |  |  |
| 4.RL.3 |  |  |  |  | • | • |  |  |  |  |  |  |  |  |  |  |  |  |  |  |
| 4.RL.4 | • |  |  |  |  |  |  |  |  |  |  |  | • |  |  | • | • | • |  |  |
| 4.RL.5 |  |  |  |  |  |  |  |  |  | • |  | • |  |  |  |  |  |  |  |  |
| 4.RL.6 |  |  |  |  |  |  |  |  |  |  |  |  |  |  |  |  |  |  |  |  |
| 4.RL.7 |  |  |  |  |  |  |  |  |  |  |  |  |  |  |  |  |  |  |  |  |
| 4.RL.9 |  |  |  |  |  |  |  |  |  |  |  |  |  |  |  |  |  |  |  |  |
| 4.RL.10 |  |  |  |  | • | • |  |  | • |  | • |  | • |  |  |  | • |  |  |  |
| 4.RI.1 |  |  |  | • |  | • |  | • |  |  |  |  |  |  |  |  |  |  |  |  |
| 4.RI.2 |  |  |  |  |  | • |  |  |  |  |  |  |  |  |  |  |  |  |  |  |
| 4.RI.3 |  |  |  |  |  |  |  | • |  |  |  |  |  |  |  |  |  |  |  |  |
| 4.RI.4 |  |  | • | • |  |  |  |  |  |  |  |  |  |  |  |  |  |  |  |  |
| 4.RI.5 |  |  |  |  |  | • |  |  |  |  | • |  |  |  |  | • |  |  |  |  |
| 4.RI.6 |  |  |  |  |  |  |  |  |  |  |  |  | • |  |  |  |  |  |  |  |
| 4.RI.7 |  |  |  |  |  |  |  | • |  |  |  |  |  |  |  |  |  |  |  |  |
| 4.RI.8 |  |  |  |  |  |  |  |  |  |  |  |  |  | • |  |  |  |  |  |  |
| 4.RI.9 |  |  |  |  |  |  |  |  |  |  |  |  |  |  |  |  |  |  |  |  |
| 4.RI.10 |  |  |  | • |  | • | • | • |  |  |  | • |  |  | • |  |  |  |  | • |
| 4.RF.3 | • | • |  | • | • | • | • | • |  | • |  | • | • | • |  | • | • | • | • |  |
| 4.RF.4 | • | • |  | • |  |  |  |  |  |  |  |  |  |  |  |  |  |  |  |  |
| 4.W.1 |  | • |  | • | • |  | • | • | • |  | • | • | • | • | • | • | • | • | • | • |
| 4.W.2 | • |  |  |  | • | • | • | • | • | • | • | • | • | • | • | • | • | • | • | • |
| 4.W.3 |  | • |  |  | • | • |  |  |  |  |  | • | • |  | • | • |  |  | • | • |
| 4.W.4 |  |  | • |  |  |  |  |  |  |  |  |  |  |  |  |  |  |  |  |  |
| 4.W.5 |  |  |  |  |  |  |  |  |  | • |  |  |  |  |  | • |  |  |  |  |
| 4.W.6 |  |  |  |  |  |  |  |  |  |  |  |  |  |  |  |  |  |  |  |  |
| 4.W.7 |  |  |  |  |  |  |  |  |  |  |  |  |  |  |  |  |  |  |  |  |
| 4.W.8 |  |  |  |  |  |  |  |  |  |  |  |  |  |  |  |  |  |  |  |  |
| 4.W.9 |  |  |  |  |  |  |  |  |  |  |  |  |  |  |  |  |  |  |  |  |
| 4.W.10 |  |  |  |  |  |  |  |  |  |  |  |  |  |  |  |  |  |  |  |  |
| 4.L.1 | • | • | • | • | • | • | • | • | • | • | • | • | • | • | • | • | • | • | • | • |
| 4.L.2 | • | • | • | • | • | • | • | • | • | • | • | • | • | • | • | • | • | • | • | • |
| 4.L.3 |  | • | • | • |  | • | • |  | • | • | • |  |  | • | • |  |  | • | • |  |
| 4.L.4 | • | • | • | • | • |  | • | • | • |  | • |  | • |  | • | • | • | • |  | • |
| 4.L.5 | • | • | • | • | • | • | • | • | • |  | • |  | • |  | • | • | • | • |  | • |
| 4.L.6 |  |  |  |  | • |  | • | • | • | • | • |  | • | • | • | • | • | • | • | • |

W = Week

# Common Core State Standards Alignment Matrix

| Standards | W21 | W22 | W23 | W24 | W25 | W26 | W27 | W28 | W29 | W30 | W31 | W32 | W33 | W34 | W35 | W36 | W37 | W38 | W39 | W40 |
|---|---|---|---|---|---|---|---|---|---|---|---|---|---|---|---|---|---|---|---|---|
| 4.RL.1 | | | | | | | | | | | | | | | | | | | | |
| 4.RL.2 | | | | | | | ● | | ● | ● | | | ● | | | | | | | |
| 4.RL.3 | | | | | | | | | | | | | | | | | | | | |
| 4.RL.4 | | | | | ● | ● | ● | ● | ● | ● | | | ● | | ● | ● | ● | ● | ● | ● |
| 4.RL.5 | ● | | | | | | | | ● | ● | | | | ● | ● | ● | ● | ● | ● | |
| 4.RL.6 | | | | | | | | | | | ● | | | | | | | | | |
| 4.RL.7 | | | | | | | | | | | | | | | | | | | | |
| 4.RL.9 | | | | | | | | | | | | | | | | | | | | |
| 4.RL.10 | | | | | | | ● | | ● | ● | | | ● | | | | | | | |
| 4.RI.1 | | | | | | | | | | | | | | | | | | | | ● |
| 4.RI.2 | | | | | ● | ● | ● | ● | | | ● | ● | ● | | ● | ● | ● | ● | ● | ● |
| 4.RI.3 | | | | | | | | | | | | | | | | | | | | |
| 4.RI.4 | | | | | ● | ● | ● | ● | ● | ● | ● | ● | | | | | | | | |
| 4.RI.5 | | | | | ● | ● | ● | ● | ● | ● | ● | ● | ● | ● | ● | ● | ● | ● | ● | ● |
| 4.RI.6 | | | | | | | | | | | | | | | | | | | | |
| 4.RI.7 | | | | | | | ● | ● | | ● | | | | | ● | | | ● | | |
| 4.RI.8 | | | | | | | | | | | | | | | | | | | | |
| 4.RI.9 | | | | | | | | | | | | | | | | | | | | |
| 4.RI.10 | | | | | ● | ● | ● | ● | | | ● | ● | ● | | ● | ● | ● | ● | ● | ● |
| 4.RF.3 | ● | ● | | ● | ● | ● | ● | ● | ● | ● | ● | ● | ● | ● | ● | ● | ● | ● | ● | ● |
| 4.RF.4 | | | | | ● | ● | ● | | ● | ● | ● | ● | ● | | | | | ● | ● | |
| 4.W.1 | | ● | | ● | | | ● | | | | ● | | | | ● | ● | | | | |
| 4.W.2 | ● | ● | ● | ● | ● | ● | ● | | | | ● | ● | | | | | | | | ● |
| 4.W.3 | ● | ● | ● | | ● | ● | ● | ● | | ● | ● | ● | ● | ● | ● | ● | ● | ● | ● | ● |
| 4.W.4 | | | ● | | | ● | ● | ● | ● | ● | | | | | | | | | | |
| 4.W.5 | | ● | | ● | | | | | | | | | | | | | | | | |
| 4.W.6 | | | | | | | | | | | | | | | | | | | | |
| 4.W.7 | | | | | | | | | | | | | | | | | | | | |
| 4.W.8 | | | | | | | | | | | | | | | | | | | | |
| 4.W.9 | | | | | | | | | | | | | | | | | | | | |
| 4.W.10 | | | | | | ● | | | | | | ● | | | | | | | | |
| 4.L.1 | ● | ● | ● | ● | ● | ● | ● | ● | ● | ● | ● | ● | ● | ● | ● | ● | ● | ● | ● | ● |
| 4.L.2 | ● | ● | ● | ● | ● | ● | ● | ● | ● | ● | ● | ● | ● | ● | ● | ● | ● | ● | ● | ● |
| 4.L.3 | ● | ● | ● | ● | | | ● | ● | ● | | ● | ● | ● | ● | ● | ● | ● | ● | ● | ● |
| 4.L.4 | ● | ● | ● | ● | ● | ● | ● | ● | ● | ● | ● | ● | ● | ● | ● | ● | ● | ● | ● | ● |
| 4.L.5 | ● | ● | ● | ● | ● | ● | ● | ● | ● | ● | ● | ● | ● | ● | ● | ● | ● | ● | ● | ● |
| 4.L.6 | ● | ● | ● | ● | | | | | | | ● | ● | | | | | | | | |

W = Week

# School to Home Communication

The research is clear that family involvement is strongly linked to student success. Support for student learning at home improves student achievement in school. Educators should not underestimate the significance of this connection.

The activities in this book create an opportunity to create or improve this school-to-home link. The activities span a week at a time and can be sent home as a weeklong homework packet each Monday. Simply clip together the strip of fun activities from the front of the book with the pages for Days 1 to 4 for the correct week.

Most of the activities can be completed independently, but many encourage feedback or interaction with a family member. The activities are simple and fun, aiming to create a brief pocket of learning that is enjoyable to all.

In order to make the school-to-home program work for students and their families, we encourage you to reach out to them with an introductory letter. Explain the program and its intent and ask them to partner with you in their children's educational process. Describe the role you expect them to play. Encourage them to offer suggestions or feedback along the way.

A sample letter is included below. Use it as is or create your own letter to introduce this project and elicit their collaboration.

---

Dear Families,

I anticipate a productive and exciting year of learning and look forward to working with you and your child. We have a lot of work to do! I hope we—teacher, student, and family—can work together as a team to achieve the goal of academic progress we all hope for this year.

I will send home a packet of homework each week on _____. There will be two items to complete each day: a single task on a strip plus a full page of focused practice. Each page or strip is labeled Day 1 (for Monday), Day 2, Day 3, or Day 4. There is no homework on Friday.

Please make sure that your student brings back the completed work _____. It is important that these are brought in on time as we may work on some of the lessons as a class.

If you have any questions about this program or would like to talk to me about it, please feel free to call or email me. Thank you for joining me in making this the best year ever for your student!

Sincerely,

_____
Name

_____
Phone

_____
Email

---

| | Day 1 | Day 2 | Day 3 | Day 4 |
|---|---|---|---|---|
| **Week 1** | Choose a favorite story or drama that you have read recently. Name two characters from the story. Describe the characters' traits and how they are similar and different. | Check your reading rate. Find a page in a book you are reading. Set a timer for one minute and start reading. At the end of the minute, count the number of words you read. | Write in your journal for 15 minutes. Think of a list of topics and write them down on the back page for when you need more journal writing ideas. | Create word family circles for the word families by placing each word part in the center and writing rhyming words in the family around it. **-ide   -all** **-ind   -ike** |
| **Week 2** | Draw a chart to put the events of a story that you have read recently in their proper sequence. Show what happened first, next, and last. | Write homophones such as *pear/pair* and *wait/weight* on bingo cards and index cards. Draw cards and read matches until someone has bingo. | Write a rebus story of a familiar nursery rhyme or fairy tale. Substitute some of the key words in the story (characters, nouns, or verbs) with small pictures. Read your rebus story to a family member. | Name an object in the room. Have someone else name another object that starts with the ending sound of the first object. The last person to be able to add a word wins. |
| **Week 3** | Ask a family member to tell you a true story about something that happened to her. Tell the main idea and share a few key details. Ask questions to find out more. | Choose two words to look up in the dictionary and compare the entries word meanings, origins, parts of speech, and pronunciations. Use the words in the same sentence. | Fold a sheet of paper into four columns and write different settings at the tops, such as forest or hospital. List words to describe each setting. Then, read your lists and ask someone to guess the settings. | Write these roots on a tic-tac-toe board: *train, move, help, like, real, lay, sleep, light, turn*. Play tic-tac-toe. Mark a root with *X* or *O* when you can add a prefix or suffix to make a new word. |
| **Week 4** | Choose a character in a story you have read recently. Fold a sheet of paper into six squares labeled *Description, Actions, Feelings, Thoughts, Quotes,* and *Goals*. Fill in the details about the character. | Write categories (food, feelings, places, etc.) on index cards. Take turns drawing a card. List as many things as you can in that category. The player with the most words in the category wins. | Illustrate and write about one of the following topics: <br>–my favorite game <br>–my best memory <br>–my best vacation <br>–my favorite book <br>–my best friend <br>–my favorite animal | Create word lists using the prefixes *pre-, un-, dis-,* and *mid-*. Think of at least three words for each prefix. Use each word in a sentence. |

| | Day 1 | Day 2 | Day 3 | Day 4 |
|---|---|---|---|---|
| **Week 5** | Study information on a time line. Write a paragraph summarizing it. Think about how the time line made it easy to understand the information. | Name an adjective and a noun that it describes. Use these adjectives to describe other nouns: *cheerful, dangerous, silly, purple, excited, juicy, rough, flat, bouncy, long.* | Write a tall tale about an imaginary character who does big things. Use *exaggeration* to describe how your character looks and acts, as well as the amazing things he or she does. | Interview two family members or friends about a shared event. Compare the accounts and determine which seems more factual and why. |

| | Day 1 | Day 2 | Day 3 | Day 4 |
|---|---|---|---|---|
| **Week 6** | Choose a story in which the main character had a problem. Make a chart to show who was involved, the problem, how it was solved, and alternate solutions. | Make word ladders to show different words for a similar idea. Place the words in order from top to bottom to show the degree of each synonym. | Practice voicing your opinion on a topic that is important to you. Be sure to give reasons to support your opinion. | Write compound word parts on separate index cards and place them facedown on a table. Take turns with a partner to turn over two cards at a time and try to make a compound word. |

| | Day 1 | Day 2 | Day 3 | Day 4 |
|---|---|---|---|---|
| **Week 7** | Retell a familiar story to a younger sibling or friend. Be sure to tell the story in the correct order and include the important details in your retelling. | Create a flip book of similes and metaphors. Draw a picture showing a simile or metaphor on the top of each flap and write the answer under it. | Draw a comic strip showing the sequence of a story you know. Show what happens in the beginning, middle, and end. Write dialogue in the 'bubbles' to show the characters' words and thoughts. | Look for word roots in a book, magazine, or newspaper. Mark a tally chart each time you find words with the roots *cred, graph, tele,* and *photo.* Think of other words with the same roots. |

| | Day 1 | Day 2 | Day 3 | Day 4 |
|---|---|---|---|---|
| **Week 8** | Read a news article about a recent event. Choose a quote from a person at the event. Explain how the person's viewpoint about the event is different than that of the article's author. | Write homophone riddles. For example, "This helps a boat move through the water." (sail or sale?) List the homophones in a word bank. Then, ask someone to solve the riddles. | Gather facts from books, reference materials, or the Internet to write a report about an animal. Tell where the animal lives, how it survives, and any unusual habits. | Compare a third-person and a first-person narrative. Tell how they are alike and different. Try to change the voice in one of the stories and tell it in first person or third person. |

**8**

| | Day 1 | Day 2 | Day 3 | Day 4 |
|---|---|---|---|---|
| **Week 9** | Compare the main characters in two different books. Write a new short story that has both characters in the same story. Be sure the characters keep their original traits. | Copy some words from a book or magazine to learn about word affixes. Decide if each word has a prefix, a suffix, both, or neither. Think of more words that follow the same patterns. | Choose a page from your journal to turn into a fictional story. Finish the story and share it with a family member to get feedback. Make corrections and then illustrate and publish your story. | Create matching pairs of antonyms and synonyms on index cards. Flip over two cards at a time to try to make a match, correctly telling if the words are antonyms or synonyms. |
| **Week 10** | Draw a picture of a main character in a story's setting. Hide details about the character in the background, such as how the character looks, what he or she does, and what happens to the character. | Research a topic. Create a word web to classify ideas and details about the topic. Make each circle of the web a different idea or category. Then, fill in the web with any facts you learn. | Choose and research a topic. Create a diagram or poster with the main points you learned. Practice telling about your poster to an audience of family members. | Create a flip book of word meanings. Look up the definitions of new words. List each word on the top of a flap, write its definition, and draw a small illustration under it. |
| **Week 11** | Read a nonfiction book. How is the text structured? Decide whether the details are presented in a time order, question/answer, problem/solution, or cause/effect format. | Design a game board. Write Fact or Opinion in each square. As players move, they make statements that are either fact or opinion. Players then vote on whether each player can move to the next space. | Write prepositional phrases on strips. Establish the setting a story and then pull a phrase strip. Write a sentence in your story using the phrase. Pull a new phrase for each paragraph. | Guess the rhyming pairs that go with these descriptions. Then, make up some of your own!<br>– large truck<br>– little insect<br>– unhappy father<br>– pretend dessert<br>– lunar song |
| **Week 12** | Read two stories on the same topic or by the same author. Tell what they have in common and what things are different. Then, choose your favorite and reread it. | Look through a book and choose three of your favorite words. List each word and its meaning, where you found it, and why you chose it. Use your words in sentences or in a story. | Write a persuasive letter making a request to someone. Explain why your idea is a good one. Edit your letter and then deliver it. | Cut from an old magazine pictures that can be described using words with the following suffixes: -est, -able, -ful, -ly. |

| | Day 1 | Day 2 | Day 3 | Day 4 |
|---|---|---|---|---|
| **Week 13** | Read an adventure story. Then, make a flowchart to show how the events unfold in the story. Explain your chart by retelling the story to a family member. | Read some familiar proverbs and explain what they mean with real-world examples. Then, try to make up a proverb. See if anyone in your family understands its meaning. | Choose a part of a story and change it. Rewrite the story so that the character acts differently, the setting or plot changes, or the story ending changes. | Write words with multiple meanings on strips. Take turns with a partner drawing words and using them in sentences. Both players must use the same word in sentences with different meanings. |

| | Day 1 | Day 2 | Day 3 | Day 4 |
|---|---|---|---|---|
| **Week 14** | Read a story. Then, act out a scene from the book for a family member. Describe the similarities and differences in your version and the story. | List 10 homographs on one side of index cards and their definitions on the others. Have a family member choose a card. Read the word aloud and have him tell you the correct definition. | Write a poem that includes rhythm or rhyme. Use descriptive words and imagery to create interest. Illustrate and publish your poem for others to read. | Draw a tree. Write a word root in the center of it. On its branches, write related words that contain or use the root. Use a dictionary or thesaurus to help you. |

| | Day 1 | Day 2 | Day 3 | Day 4 |
|---|---|---|---|---|
| **Week 15** | Look in a magazine. Find the main idea of a science article. Explain any charts or visuals that helped you understand the meaning of the text. Tell why you think the author included them. | Choose five words from a book you are reading. Have family members guess each word by giving clues about the meaning of the word, sounds in the word, number of syllables, or its synonym or antonym. | Write a set of directions telling how to do something. Include a diagram or illustration to help the reader understand. Have a partner try to follow your directions. Make changes as needed. | Write down four pairs of commonly confused words such as *loose/lose*. For each word in the pair, write a sentence using the word correctly and draw a picture. |

| | Day 1 | Day 2 | Day 3 | Day 4 |
|---|---|---|---|---|
| **Week 16** | Go on a genre scavenger hunt. Look through shelves at your local library or your bookshelf at home. Tally the number of books you see in each genre such as fiction, mystery, and poetry. | Play a punctuation sound effects game. Read a passage aloud. Assign a sound to each type of punctuation. For example, click your tongue for a period or say "ch-ch" for quotation marks. | Write two versions of a short adventure story using third person voice in one version and first person voice in the other. Have a family member read both versions and choose the one she likes best. | On one side of an index card, write a riddle that describes a word. Use roots such as *port*, *ped*, *phone*, or *dict*. Ask, "What word am I?" Let someone try to guess your riddles. |

| | Day 1 | Day 2 | Day 3 | Day 4 |
|---|---|---|---|---|
| **Week 17** | Read a few pages of a story and stop to make a prediction just before some action takes place. Write the page number and your prediction. Read on to see if your prediction is correct. | Choose five everyday objects. Make up sentences with each object that use personification. For example, "The couch groaned with the dog's weight." | Write in your journal about a true event. Use signal words to show transitions as you write, such as *therefore*, *in addition*, *as a result*, and any others you may think of. | Make bingo cards with different synonyms. Call out each synonym to friends or family members. Have them mark the synonyms on their cards. Play until there is a winner. |
| **Week 18** | Read two articles about the same topic. Tell how they are alike and different. Then, illustrate a cover page for each article, showing some of the main ideas in each illustration. | Tell a friend about a favorite game. Then, tell a neighbor what you did in school. Notice the way you spoke to your friend using casual speech, while the other was likely more formal. | Read an article and write a short report about it. In your report, pretend to interview the author, asking any questions you may have about the article. | Write several nouns on index cards. Draw cards and take turns saying three describing words. As someone guesses the object, he gets the card. The player with the most cards wins the game. |
| **Week 19** | Check your reading speed. Choose any text. Set the timer and note how many unrelated words you can read in one minute. Do not read sentences, just single words. Write down your score. | Write four run-on sentences or sentence fragments while a partner does the same. Then, exchange papers and correct each other's mistakes. | With a family member's help, use the computer or another device to write a message to someone you know by text or email. Be sure to use correct spelling, punctuation, and capitalization. | Read a difficult passage. Then, close the book and open it to any page. Choose three unfamiliar words and guess their meaning by looking at them in context. |
| **Week 20** | Stop reading at a few points in a story. In three columns, write about what is happening, what you infer or think might happen, and what you know from your experience that led you to that inference. | Choose an article from a newspaper or a news magazine. Highlight the pronouns in different colors, depending on their type (personal, possessive, interrogative). | Write an adventure story in which the reader can choose a direction to follow. At key stopping points, direct the reader to follow page *A* or *B*. Then, offer two different endings to the story. | Make up idiom riddles by leaving blank spaces for key words. For example, "It's raining _____ and dogs." Ask a partner to guess the missing words. |

| | Day 1 | Day 2 | Day 3 | Day 4 |
|---|---|---|---|---|
| **Week 21** | Create a title for a newspaper article about an event that happened to you. Then, list four or five headings that you would put in the article to help the reader uncover what happened. | Make up a silly story game, leaving blank spaces in a story for nouns, verbs, and adjectives to replace with your own choices or those of a friend. Then, read the stories you created. | Write a travel journal about a place you'd like to visit. Look for information in brochures, books, or online. Describe the places, activities, weather, geography, and people found at your destination. | Write these affixes and their meanings on separate index cards: *pre-* (before), *re-* (again), *un-* (not), *-less* (without), *-able* (can be), *-er* (one who). Then, use the cards to play a matching game. |
| **Week 22** | Read a short play. Make a poster that shows the features of drama—how it is staged, the number of acts and scenes, the characters, and a few stage directions. Use your poster to retell the play. | Choose a hero and create a tower of characteristics about that person. Starting at the bottom of the tower, list the characteristics and deeds of your hero until you reach the top. | Write a short play. List the characters and set the stage with opening directions. Then, write lines of dialogue for each actor in the play. Find friends and family to act out your play. | Make a word web. Place a word in a center circle and then draw bubbles around it. Fill in each bubble with a related word or phrase, synonym, antonym, paired word, or description of the center word. |
| **Week 23** | Tell a family member about a time you were brave. Then, make up a tall tale about the event where you are the hero or heroine and retell with actions and exaggeration. | Write five vocabulary words on index cards. Look for relationships based on their meanings, patterns, sounds, or spellings. Sort the cards and add more words to each category. | Write a short mystery that begins, "It was a dark and stormy night . . ." Use descriptive words and imagery in your story. | Choose five science vocabulary words to define and illustrate. Explain your drawings to a family member. |
| **Week 24** | Think of two myths or legends you have read. Compare the legends and the characteristics of the hero or heroine in each one. Describe your favorite word to a family member and why you like it best. | Guess the meaning of these phrases that originate from myths: "Cupid's arrow," "the Midas touch," "Herculean strength." Then, ask a family member to explain and give an example. | Choose a famous person in history and find facts in books or on the Internet. Write three interesting facts about the person. Share your findings with a family member. | Copy a descriptive sentence and cut out each word. Scramble the words and reorder the adjectives and phrases to create a new sentence. Add transition words or conjunctions as needed. |

| | Day 1 | Day 2 | Day 3 | Day 4 |
|---|---|---|---|---|
| **Week 25** | Continue this story: Kay and Jack got off the bus and walked through the front door. "Oh, no!" Kay cried. "Not again!" | Go on a scavenger hunt around your home. How many things can you find that begin with the first letter of your first name? Write a list. | List as many words as you can think of that have the same vowel sound as *scream*. | Look at this list of adjectives: *red*, *huge*, *flat*, *loud*, *warm*, *shiny*. Find at least one thing in your home or neighborhood that can be described by each of these words. |
| **Week 26** | Search your home for things that have only one syllable. How many can you find? | Use books, magazines, or the Internet to learn about your favorite animal. Write one paragraph about that animal. | Write each letter of the alphabet on an index card. Shuffle the cards. Pull the first two off of the pile. Think of a word that includes those two letters. Continue until you finish the deck of cards. | Think about this idiom: "between a rock and a hard place." Draw a picture illustrating this idiom. |
| **Week 27** | Write six prefixes on separate index cards. Lay them facedown. Each time you flip over a card, write at least three words with that prefix. | Make bingo cards with different antonyms. Call out each antonym to friends or family members. Have them mark the antonyms on their cards. Play until there is a winner. | Think of your favorite character from a book or story. What are five adjectives that describe this character? | Write each vowel on an index card. Lay the cards facedown. Select two. Think of a word that uses those two letters. |
| **Week 28** | Write six suffixes on separate index cards. Lay them facedown. Each time you flip over a card, write at least three words with that suffix. | Write three adjectives to describe something in your bedroom. Write three antonyms for each word. Use a thesaurus if you need help. | Find a comic strip. Write your own dialogue to replace what the writer has written. | As quickly as you can, write down 10 words that begin with the letter *m*. Use a dictionary if you need help. |

| | Day 1 | Day 2 | Day 3 | Day 4 |
|---|---|---|---|---|
| **Week 29** | Continue this story: "We're really going to be in trouble this time," Sunil said to Ajay. The two brothers stared at each other, completely frozen. | Search your home for things with names that have at least two syllables. How many things can you find? Make a list. | Create flash cards, each with a different coordinating conjunction. Flip over each card and then use that coordinating conjunction in a sentence. | Make bingo cards with different nouns. Call out each noun. Have friends or family members find the noun on their cards. Play until there is a winner. |

| | Day 1 | Day 2 | Day 3 | Day 4 |
|---|---|---|---|---|
| **Week 30** | Go on a scavenger hunt around your home. How many things can you find that begin with a vowel? Make a list. | Create a word search with synonyms for *run*. Use a thesaurus to help you. Have a friend or family member help you try to find 20 synonyms. Make a list. | List as many words as you can think of that rhyme with *book*. Make a list. | Think about this idiom: "Too many cooks spoil the broth." Draw a picture illustrating this idiom. |

| | Day 1 | Day 2 | Day 3 | Day 4 |
|---|---|---|---|---|
| **Week 31** | What is your favorite hobby or sport? Write a paragraph about it. Explain why you enjoy it. | Make bingo cards with prefixes and suffixes. Call out each affix. Have friends or family members find the affix on their cards. Play until there is a winner. | As quickly as you can, write 10 words that begin with the letter *l*. Use a dictionary if you need help. | Create flash cards with boring words such as *nice* and *bad*. With a partner, use the flash cards to come up with more interesting synonyms. |

| | Day 1 | Day 2 | Day 3 | Day 4 |
|---|---|---|---|---|
| **Week 32** | How many words can you think of that have double letters? Write as many as you can. | Go on a scavenger hunt around your home. How many things can you find that begin with the first letter of your last name? Make a list. | Create a word search with antonyms for *mean*. Use a thesaurus if you need help. Have a friend or family member find all of the words. Make a list. | Use books, magazines, or the Internet to learn about an animal you know nothing about. Write three interesting things about the animal. |

| | Day 1 | Day 2 | Day 3 | Day 4 |
|---|---|---|---|---|
| **Week 33** | Continue this story: "What did you say?" Zoe asked, amazed. She couldn't believe what she'd just heard. | On cards, write words that have suffixes. Cut apart the cards so that the roots and suffixes are separated. Mix up the cards. Have a friend or family member rebuild the words. | Read a newspaper or magazine article. How many first- and second-hand accounts can you find? Circle the words that reveal if the story is a first- or second-hand account. | Create a crossword puzzle with synonyms for *shout*. Have a friend or family member try to solve your puzzle. Make a list. |
| **Week 34** | Go on a scavenger hunt around your home. How many things can you find that have the long or short /o/ sound? Make a list. | Think about this idiom: "A bird in the hand is worth two in the bush." Draw a picture illustrating this idiom. | Find stories in newspapers and magazines for each kind of text structure, such as problem/solution, cause/effect, etc. | Create a word search with words that use prefixes. Have a friend or family member try to find all of the words. |
| **Week 35** | List as many words as you can think of that have the same vowel sound as heard in *house*? Make a list. | Create a crossword puzzle with synonyms for *happy*. Have a friend or family member try to solve your puzzle. Make a list. | Use books, magazines, or the Internet to learn about a museum you would like to visit someday. Write three interesting things about the museum. Share your findings with a friend. | Write three adjectives to describe something in your home. Then, think of three synonyms for each word. Use a thesaurus if you need help. |
| **Week 36** | As quickly as you can, write down five words that begin with each vowel. Use a dictionary if you need help. | Create a word search with linking words and phrases. Have a friend or family member find all of the words and phrases. | Play "idiom charades." Act out an idiom for a partner. Then, have your partner act out an idiom for you. Did either of you guess correctly? | Continue this drama: **Eduardo**: What do you think is in there? **Sheila**: I don't know, but I'm going to find out. Oops! |

| | Day 1 | Day 2 | Day 3 | Day 4 |
|---|---|---|---|---|
| **Week 37** | Continue this story: Dominic and Carl had really been looking forward to the camping trip—until now. | On cards, write words that have suffixes. Cut apart the cards so that the roots and suffixes are separated. Mix up the cards. Have a friend or family member rebuild the words. | Search your home for things that have the long or short *e* sound. How many can you find? Make a list. | As quickly as you can, write five words that begin with the letter *v*. Use a dictionary if you need help. |

| | Day 1 | Day 2 | Day 3 | Day 4 |
|---|---|---|---|---|
| **Week 38** | Create a word search with words that use suffixes. Have a friend or family member find all of the words. | What is the best book or story you have ever read? Write a paragraph explaining why. Give reasons to support your opinion. | Think about this idiom: "Go out on a limb." Draw a picture illustrating this idiom. | Create a crossword puzzle with action verbs. Have a friend or family member solve your puzzle. |

| | Day 1 | Day 2 | Day 3 | Day 4 |
|---|---|---|---|---|
| **Week 39** | List as many words as you can think of that have the same vowel sound as *tray*. Make a list. | Write five adjectives to describe what you're wearing right now. | Go on a scavenger hunt around your home. How many things can you find that begin with the letter *c*? Make a list. | Write these words on index cards: *sale, sure, ate, night, hire, close*. Write each word's homophone on the back of the card. |

| | Day 1 | Day 2 | Day 3 | Day 4 |
|---|---|---|---|---|
| **Week 40** | As quickly as you can, write five words that have at least three syllables. Use a dictionary if you need help. | List as many words as you can think of that rhyme with *tough*. Make a list. | Continue this drama: **Shelby**: I can't believe it! This can't be happening! **Anna**: What? What's wrong? | Write idioms on one set of index cards and the meanings on another. Have a partner do the same. Trade sets. Match each idiom to its meaning. |

Underline the complete sentences.

Ben to the shops to get lunch. He was surprised to meet two of his friends at the counter. Three weeks ago. They saw a movie together at the theater. Ben asked, "Are there any new movies out this week?" Did not remember. They decided to look online for showtimes. One of the movies very exciting.

You can use adjectives to give the reader more information about (nouns, verbs).

Place a dot (•) between syllables.

r e v i e w

r e m a i n d e r

r e w o r d

Circle phrases with adjectives that are in the correct order.

**striped large cat**

**bouncy little puppy**

**new blue bicycle**

**yellow old bucket**

Complete the synonym.

**fury**

r__ __e

Circle the nouns. Underline the adjectives.

The yellow cab pulled up to the curb. A nicely dressed couple stepped out of the cab and walked down the crowded sidewalk. The noise from the traffic was deafening, but they didn't mind. It was an ordinary day.

Every Saturday morning, May helped her family do chores around the house. They would dust the furniture, sweep the floors, and scrub the bathtub. Then, they would wash, dry, and fold the clothes that needed to be washed. Once the laundry was finished, they would put all of the clean clothes into dresser drawers or hang them in closets. When they were finished, May always felt very **weary** but **satisfied** from doing all of that hard work.

**Weary** means _____ .

**tired      bored      upset**

**Satisfied** means _____ .

**anxious      contented      flustered**

○ **weather**

○ **whether**

Ate the entire plate of spaghetti in five minutes.

**complete sentence      fragment**

Correct the sentence.

"Don´t worry she whispered.

---

Which sentence is missing a subject?

○ **Of all state capitals, Augusta is the farthest east.**

○ **The town of Berwick, Maine, is almost 400 years old.**

○ **Every summer, welcomes many travelers to its parks and beaches.**

---

Circle the prepositional phrases.

**after the swim meet**

**because you were sleeping**

**under the umbrella**

**although my cat sleeps a lot**

---

Place a ✓ by each synonym.

**sad**

❑ down

❑ gloomy

❑ worry

❑ unhappy

❑ cheery

❑ cry

---

Count the complete sentences. _____

   My bedroom is at the top of the stairs. Make a right to get to the attic door. Will be right in front of you. Three stairs from the top. It is probably dusty up there.

---

Correct the sentence.

Mr Lebowitz said Thank you for mowing my

lawn Javon.

---

Place a ✓ by each antonym.

**sad**

❑ sure

❑ jolly

❑ laugh

❑ loving

❑ bright

❑ joyful

---

Sort the verbs.

**went   have   spins   typed   swam   dream   is   kept**

| present | past |
|---------|------|
|         |      |

---

**cooperate**

○ to find something

○ to work together

○ to try anytime

---

**18**

Charlie had some bad (luck, lucky) today.

He lost his (luck, lucky) hat in a gust of wind.

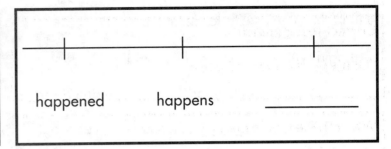

happened          happens          _____

---

Underline the fragment in this paragraph. Then, rewrite the fragment as a complete sentence.

    Last summer, we saw a caterpillar in the woods. Was green and had thorns, just like a prickly plant. Alejandra said that many caterpillars look like plants to blend in with their surroundings. This way, they are less likely to be picked out by predators.

_____

_____

_____

_____

---

Walks to school every Tuesday morning.

○ **sentence**

○ **fragment**

---

Correct the mistakes.

"Will you go to the game

tonight?"

"No. I has to go to the store.

Can Grace go?"

"She think she can come. I'll let

you know."

---

Write a two-syllable word that has the same vowel sound as **tune**.

---

○ **rare**

○ **rair**

○ **reire**

---

Circle the **pear**.

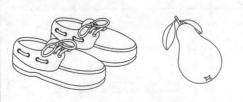

---

misdeed = bad act

miscount = bad tally

misbehavior = _____

Fill in the blanks with forms of **be**.

Jingyi will _____ at the gym tonight. The first soccer practice of the year _____ scheduled for tonight. Her team _____ very good last year, but now Jingyi _____ worried about how they will do.

Circle the word(s) that rhyme with **raise**.

There were delays at the airport today. It was a maze near our gate. Our flight was canceled. Tomorrow, we will have to retrace our steps.

Some wild leopards hunt large animals such as gorillas.

**complete sentence          fragment**

Choose the topic sentence.

○ **Border collies weigh about 45 pounds and are black and white.**

○ **Border collies are one of the most intelligent breeds of dogs in the world.**

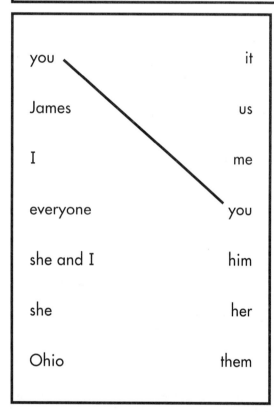

| | |
|---|---|
| you | it |
| James | us |
| I | me |
| everyone | you |
| she and I | him |
| she | her |
| Ohio | them |

Spell the word correctly.

**beettle**

_____

As quickly as he could, Owen slipped the collar over his dog's neck. "Come on, Lizzy," he said. Lizzy scratched at the collar with her back paw, but Owen took no notice. He was too distracted. This will be a short walk around the block, he decided. But, Lizzy had other plans.

What do you think will happen next?

_____

_____

_____

_____

_____

_____

**misfortune (n.)**

○ bad sale

○ bad luck

○ bad song

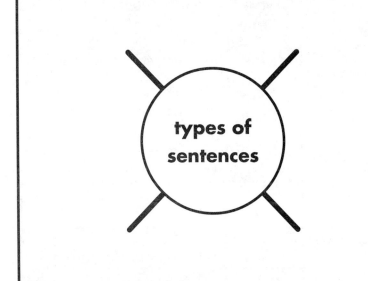

types of
sentences

Synonyms (always, do not always)
have the same exact meaning as
each other.

Place a dot (•) between syllables.

w e s t e r n

m a n t e l p i e c e

s i s t e r l y

Complete the
prepositional
phrases.
An airplane can fly
_____ the sky.
A whale can swim
_____ the sea.
A hiker can climb
_____ a mountain.
A horse can gallop
_____ the field.

○ **guste**

○ **guest**

○ **geust**

Circle the stronger sentence.

**We got a fossil!**

**We dug up a fossil!**

Do you wear your own clothes or a uniform to school? Which is
better? Give reasons to support your opinion.

_____

_____

_____

_____

_____

_____

The **predicate** of a
sentence contains
a verb.

○ **true**

○ **false**

_____ to Theaters This Autumn!

**Comming**          **Coming**          **Comeing**

Correct the sentence.

Have you ever bin to north Carolina

---

Which sentence gives an opinion?

○ **No one is certain when the new town hall will open.**

○ **The new town hall was too pricey and does not help the community.**

○ **Citizens are welcome to voice their opinions at a meeting this Tuesday.**

---

Rewrite the fragments as complete sentences.

The first day of the year.

_____

_____

Watched the bird feeder.

_____

_____

---

Place a ✓ by each synonym.

**wash**

❑ bathe

❑ clean

❑ blank

❑ dishes

❑ scrub

❑ new

---

The butcher's shop around the corner.

This sentence is missing a _____.

**subject          predicate**

---

Take an umbrella in case it rains.

**sentence          fragment**

---

Place a ✓ by each antonym.

**wash**

❑ hold

❑ stain

❑ smear

❑ foul

❑ ignore

❑ dirt

---

you   →
them

me   ↓
us

| | | | Y | O | U | R | S |

---

**elegant**

○ cheerful

○ hopeful

○ graceful

---

I have (there, their) home address written down.

Have you been (there, their) before?

---

Four of my cousins live in St. Louis. I hope to visit them soon.

Which underlined word/phrase is a subject?

_____

---

Circle **S** for a sentence or **F** for a fragment.

| | | |
|---|---|---|
| Abby hurried to finish her work. | S | F |
| Don't forget your bag. | S | F |
| Bought the shirt online. | S | F |
| Did they find their tickets? | S | F |
| Plays the trombone. | S | F |
| The easiest piece of homework. | S | F |
| Did not see David there. | S | F |

---

_____ one of you is coming?

_____ is visiting you today?

To _____ am I speaking?

---

Circle the similes.

She was as sweet as pie.

He was a happy camper.

He was a shining star.

She was cold as ice to her friend.

He ate like a pig at dinner.

---

Fill in the blanks with pronouns.

_____ (David) carried _____

(the plate of pancakes) over to

_____ (his sick mother).

---

Complete the synonym.

**delight**

g____e____

---

Correct the sentence.

"Where are they going with that board," Brook asked?

---

misread = read incorrectly

misuse = use in the wrong way

misspell = _____

---

**23**

We spent New Year's with family in Fairbanks, Alaska. It was my first time up north during the winter. The sun set as early as 3:00 in the afternoon! I made a wish each time it set.

This paragraph mainly (tells a story, teaches about a place).

Rewrite the sentence correctly.

i orderred ham and eggs for breckfast this morning

_____

_____

I _____ catch the train on time, or I _____ _____ asking someone for a ride.

Please walk to school with me this Tuesday.

○ **sentence**

○ **fragment**

Blake and Keisha did not expect to enjoy the play. In the beginning, it seemed a bit dull, but by the second act, they were **glued to their seats**.

What does the idiom mean?

_____

_____

_____

_____

_____

Spell the word correctly.

**kingdome**

_____

Write about something you love. Why do you love it?

_____

_____

_____

_____

_____

_____

_____

_____

**mislead (v.)**

○ lead the wrong way

○ not lead

○ let others lead

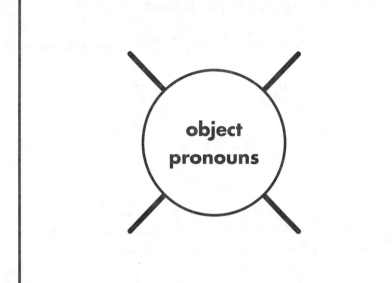

object
pronouns

A compound sentence (has, joins)

two simple sentences.

**Misplace** means

_____

_____

_____.

---

Circle words or phrases that need to be capitalized.

**south dakota**

**local library**

**new york**

**town mayor**

**mississippi river**

**state capital**

---

Spell the word correctly.

**loveley**

_____

---

| brave | → | **bravery** |
| warm | → | _____ |
| happy | → | _____ |
| absent | → | _____ |

---

Use **and**, **but**, or **or** to join the sentences.

I wanted to go to the racetrack. It was closed for the season.

_____

_____

Do you like vanilla cakes? Would you rather have chocolate with vanilla icing?

_____

_____

---

◯ **bread**

◯ **bred**

---

The fish are in their tanks, but I don´t see the frog anywhere!

**simple sentence**          **compound sentence**

The jelly jars and cans of beans.

**sentence          fragment**

---

Combine the sentences.

Jayden and I ran the cake up to the Morenos´ apartment. Sona brought the grab bags.

_____

_____

---

Circle the correct sentence.

The quick brown fox stopped suddenly.

The brown quick fox stopped suddenly.

The shiny copper kettle whistled loudly from the stovetop.

The copper shiny kettle whistled loudly from the stovetop.

---

Place a ✓ by each synonym.

**walk**

☐ ride

☐ pace

☐ stroll

☐ hurried

☐ stride

☐ hike

---

Count the articles. _____

The first bell of the school day rings at 7:55. All students should be at their desks at this time. If a student comes in late to school, he must get a late slip from the front office.

---

Insert the missing comma.

Autumn has already started but the weather

is still nice enough to take a dip in the pool.

---

Place a ✓ by each pronoun.

☐ she

☐ he

☐ I

☐ by

☐ it

☐ and

☐ why

---

Sort the nouns.

**women´s   sheers   tongues   baker´s
fortunes   Chris´s   wolves   chief´s**

| plural | possessive |
|--------|------------|
|        |            |

---

**blend (v.)**

○ mix

○ divide things

○ paint over

Emma has a telescope, but (she, it) never looks through (her, it) anymore. I wonder what made (she, her) lose interest in it.

The frightened bird _____ so loudly, the noise pierced my ear!

**tweeted     chirped     shrieked**

Circle **S** for a sentence or **F** for a fragment.

| | | |
|---|---|---|
| The many kinds of insect. | S | F |
| Tulips bloom in the spring. | S | F |
| All of my friends are at the game. | S | F |
| Did Zoe and Patrick? | S | F |
| The tallest mountain in the world. | S | F |
| Have a sandwich! | S | F |
| The three brothers shared a room. | S | F |

The dog is _____ on the floor.

**laying     lying**

Now I _____ me down to sleep.

**lay     lie**

_____ as a button

_____ as a bird

_____ as gold

_____ as a razor

loaf × 2 = two _____

life × 2 = two _____

chief × 2 = two _____

○ **miels**

○ **miles**

○ **myles**

My teacher placed our papers _____ the desk.

I _____ the instructions and did the wrong problem set.

**misread     misspelled     mistitled**

Should cell phones be allowed in school? Give reasons to support your opinion.

_____

_____

_____

---

Circle the subject. Underline the complete predicate.

Frogs from different parts of the world

have different calls.

---

Revise the fragment.

"I can't. Too much work to finish before class."

_____

---

What is missing from this fragment?

Boarded the airplane at 10:00 in the morning.

_____

_____

_____

---

Penny wanted to make a paper-mache piñata that would look like a horse. Her friends wanted to help. Penny appreciated all of the help, but when they were finished, the horse looked more like a duck!

Which proverb or adage sums up this situation?

○ **A friend in need is a friend indeed.**

○ **Too many cooks spoil the broth.**

○ **Two hands are better than one.**

---

Complete the synonym

**rook**

s_ _o____e

---

In ancient Greek mythology, Poseidon was the god of the ocean and earthquakes. He was best known for holding a **trident**, a special spear with pointed ends. He used his trident to start storms and calm the seas.

What is the prefix of **trident**? _____

How many pointed ends does a trident have? (Hint: the prefix gives you a clue.) _____

List three other words that use the same prefix as trident.

_____   _____   _____

---

**opposit**

**opposite**

**oppasit**

---

Fill in the blanks with verbs in the correct tenses.

Ryan and Janessa _____ to Colorado to visit me. I cannot wait unit they
      *(present progressive, drive)*
arrive. We _____ to Sunset Camp to spend a few days in the mountains.
      *(future progressive, go)*
Last year we _____ on going but it rained the entire week. I sure hope the
      *(past progressive, plan)*
weather is nice while they are here. I can't wait to show them the new house my parents _____.
      *(present progressive, buy)*

---

The girl (whose, that) phone rang should answer it.

---

Place a dot (•) between syllables.

m i s t a k e n

m i s d e e d

m i s l e d

---

Circle the fragments.

At the grocery store.

We bought food for dinner.

I wanted pizza.

Salad instead.

The salad was delicious!

---

Spell the word correctly.

**mattere**

_____

---

Which sentence describes the scene more precisely?

◯ **The young woman sat on the bench waiting for the bus.**

◯ **The young woman leaned back the metal bench waiting for the bus.**

---

Write a paragraph with your opinion about a topic that is important to you. Use ideas that are connected to each other to support your opinion.

_____

_____

_____

_____

_____

---

**mishear**

◯ hear all of

◯ hear nothing

◯ hear wrongly

---

The neighbors thought they saw a **ghost**.

**subject**     **direct object**

Punctuate the sentence correctly.

What a beautiful dog you have. What is his name, and may I pet him? Carla asked her new neighbor.

Do you think computer games are good for kids? Give reasons to support your opinion.

_____

_____

_____

_____

_____

Underline the sentence fragment.

Alice and her brother each have a map to get to school. A map for Townsend School and a map for Carter School.

Place a ✓ by each synonym.

**smell**

☐ sting

☐ plugged

☐ scent

☐ odor

☐ reek

☐ stench

(Can, May, Must) you play that piano so loudly?

Insert the missing comma.

Lily and I signed up for choir but James and Katie are only playing in the band.

Place a ✓ by each correctly spelled word.

☐ roled

☐ fountain

☐ sertain

☐ equator

☐ orphen

☐ oxen

Polar bears are fearsome hunters, but **prey** is not always easy to find. In tough times, the bears will **scavenge** for any kind of food. They root through **shallow** waters, nesting sites, and even human garbage.

**Prey** means _____.

**Scavenge** means _____.

**Shallow** means _____.

Circle the prepositions.

**around**

**back**

**behind**

**among**

**bottom**

The lonely dog _____ through the night.

**barked          howled**

---

Complete the sentences with the correct verbs.

Janesha, your ice cream cone _____ all over the floor. (*past progressive, drip*)

Dad _____. (*present progressive, drive*)

---

Circle **S** for simple or **C** for compound.

| | | |
|---|---|---|
| The cities of Houston and Corpus Christi border the Gulf of Mexico. | S | C |
| The shyest puppy played on its own in the corner, but the others nipped at our legs. | S | C |
| Sam counted to 50, and the rest of us ran and hid. | S | C |
| You can make celery salt by mixing ordinary table salt with ground celery seeds. | S | C |

---

Underline the prepositional phrases.

The diamond necklace was hidden inside the box.

Jacob put his shiny tooth under the pillow.

My puppy, Blondie, is hiding behind the tree.

---

Choose the complete sentence.

○ **Run three times around the block!**

○ **Ran three times around the block.**

---

**toil (v.)**

○ work very hard

○ work very little

---

**scenere**

**scenery**

**seenery**

---

**definite = absolute**

**plenty = a _ _ _ _ d _ _ t**

---

underneath = beneath, below

underwater = below water

underground = _____

Name _____

Circle the correct auxiliary verb.

(Could, May) I please leave the table?

(Would, Might) you please pass the salt?

I (shall, should) have helped make dinner.

Circle the pronoun. Underline the noun it refers to.

Ali and Jack found two slugs, but they wouldn't go near the creatures.

I _____ doing homework all day yesterday, so I _____ play softball today.

Draw a line through the word(s) that cannot be used as nouns.

**crack**

**sunny**

**race**

**pour**

Do you agree with the adage "You are never too old to learn"? Explain.

_____

_____

_____

_____

_____

_____

_____

○ **spying**

○ **spieing**

○ **spyeing**

**underlie**

○ tell a bad lie

○ lie beneath

○ lie quietly

   The Arctic tern looks **unremarkable**. It is mostly white and gray and is not too big. Don't let its humble appearance fool you though. No animal **migrates** farther than the Arctic tern. Twice a year, Arctic terns fly thousands of miles from one **hemisphere** to the other.

What is an Arctic tern? _____

_____

What does **migrates** mean? _____

_____

What does **unremarkable** mean? _____

_____

What is a **hemisphere**? _____

_____

Underline two sentences that can be joined using coordinating conjunctions.

　　Summer was coming to end, too quickly as always. It was late August, and Jose had just celebrated his birthday. It was his 12th birthday. He didn't get very many presents. The few he got, however, he loved. He could hardly tear himself away from a new game in order to write thank-you cards.

How many syllables does **misread** have? _____

How many syllables does **shouldered** have? _____

Place a dot (•) between syllables.

l a r g e l y

b a r e l y

c a r e f u l l y

Circle the subjective pronouns.

**him**

**we**

**I**

**us**

**them**

**you**

**me**

Complete the synonym.

**almost**

a__  __ut

loud ➔ **loudest**

stormy ➔ _____

fun ➔ _____

amusing ➔ _____

How do you think your school could help the environment? Support your idea with facts and details.

_____

_____

_____

_____

_____

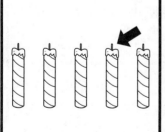

○ **fourth**

○ **forth**

Miss a Beet: Veggies _____ Run

**on The**　　**On the**　　**on the**

Correct the capitalization errors.

mount St. helens is an active Volcano in the state of washington.

What does a coordinating conjunction do?

_____

_____

List three coordinating conjunctions.

_____

_____

What does "too many cooks spoil the broth" mean?

_____

_____

_____

_____

_____

Place a ✓ by each synonym.

**talk**

❑ chatter

❑ remember

❑ open

❑ find

❑ write

❑ speak

Circle the correct phrase.

the plodding green turtle

the green plodding turtle

Tomorrow, I _____ getting up early.

Place a ✓ by each antonym.

**talk**

❑ hush

❑ write

❑ keep quiet

❑ pretend

❑ nod

❑ save

Sort the correctly and incorrectly spelled words.

**spices  trumpits  crumbled  explorers  halte allee  tryout  bluberr**

| correct | incorrect |
|---------|-----------|
|         |           |

**Wobble** means

_____

_____

_____

_____

_____.

I am on my way to (doctor, Dr.) Gupta´s office.

He has been my (doctor, Dr.) for two years.

---

Cross out the extra comma.

Reggie, and Sydney are close friends, but Reggie will have to move away at the end of the year.

---

Imagine you are writing a story about two people who get lost in the woods.

Write one detail that shows how they feel.

_____

_____

_____

How will they find their way?

_____

_____

_____

_____

---

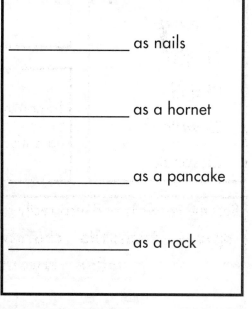

_____ did you put your backpack?

_____ are you late?
_____ are you coming?

|   |   | W |   |
|---|---|---|---|
|   | W | H |   |   |
|   |   | Y |   |

---

_____ as nails

_____ as a hornet

_____ as a pancake

_____ as a rock

---

Fill in the blanks with adverbs.

Martin _____ completed his test before the bell rang _____ at the end of the day.

---

○ **giese**

○ **geise**

○ **geese**

---

Mom roasted the potatoes _____ the oven.

---

underdressed = not dressed well enough

underdone = not cooked enough

underage = _____

Only one blank is missing the word **and**. Fill it in and leave the others blank.

Eva, _____ Claudia, and Paige could not fall asleep. They had just watched a scary movie, _____ *Night and Dismay, You Are the One.* Truthfully, _____ they weren't very scared. Still, it was fun to pretend, _____ it was even nicer to have an excuse to stay up.

---

Circle the cause. Underline the effect.

Trees grow more quickly when they get

a lot of sunlight.

---

I _____ speaking with Pam now, but I _____ talk to

you after we are finished.

---

Create prepositional phrases.

on _____

about _____

through _____

against _____

behind _____

---

People used to think that when you got to a certain age, you could no longer change or learn new things.

Which proverb or adage sums up this situation?

○ **Better late than never.**

○ **Two wrongs don't make a right.**

○ **You can't teach an old dog new tricks.**

---

Spell the word correctly.

**reatreat**

_____

---

Some people are allowed to take their pets with them to work. Do you think that is a good idea? Give reasons to support your opinion.

_____

_____

_____

_____

_____

_____

_____

---

**underfed**

○ fed bad things

○ fed too little

○ fed too much

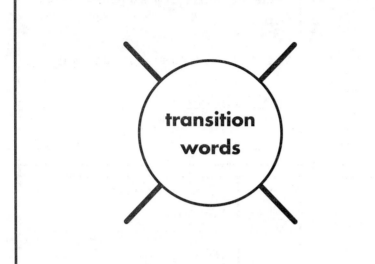

You usually learn about the setting at the (beginning, end) of a story.

**Undersea** means

_____

_____

_____ .

Complete the prepositional phrases.

_____ the tree

_____ a bush

_____ the garden

_____ a lawn

_____ the flowerpot

_____ a vegetable patch

Complete the synonym.

**dim**

___ain___

Circle the coordinating conjunction. Underline the subjects.

I have never been stung by a bee before, but Ben has been stung several times already this year.

Which is incorrect?

○ **to the store**

○ **to many books**

○ **to eat dinner**

One of our neighbors has a large olive **grove**. He planted the trees in rows and made sure they were far enough apart from each other so that each has room to grow. During the harvest season, he hires extra workers to come to the **grove** and pick the olives off of the trees.

When the olives are first picked, they are treated because they are very bitter when fresh. He then sells his olives at a local farmers market.

**Grove** means _____ .

**wide valley**          **group of trees**

The buses on the road, and the cars in the parking lot.

**complete sentence**          **fragment**

Punctuate the sentence correctly.

My grandfather was a cowboy and he used to ride a horse all day long.

---

Which sentence is an imperative?

○ **Please return the tools you borrowed.**

○ **"Pleased to meet you, Mrs. Bailey," Silvia said.**

○ **His birthday gift pleased him.**

---

Circle the simile and explain what it means.

Mrs. Kurchek was as busy as a bee.

_____

_____

_____

_____

_____

---

Place a ✓ by each synonym.

**animal**

❑ hoof

❑ wild

❑ beast

❑ live

❑ creature

❑ gorge

---

Fill in the blank with the correct relative pronoun.

The artist, _____ I called yesterday, said he would paint me.

---

Yesterday, I _____building sand castles on the beach.

---

Place a ✓ by each word with the vowel sound in **mean**.

❑ heavy

❑ imply

❑ umpire

❑ fielder

❑ liar

❑ perfect

---

Sort the words.

**ally   carelessly   rally   early   frighteningly
dearly   ashamedly   bully**

| adverb | noun |
|--------|------|
|        |      |

---

Our team won the

championship game___

In what place is your

basketball team ___

Dylan forgot to give Lia (her, hers) book.

The book has been (her, hers) since she was six years old.

---

The girls _____ at the silly joke.

**laughed     giggled**

They thought the joke was _____!

**hilarious     funny**

---

Circle the main idea. Underline a detail that supports the main idea.

Many words grow over time. Take the word *undermine*. It once meant simply to dig underground. You might undermine the earth to build (surprise!) a mine. Or, you might dig under something to make it fall. Armies used to do this. They would "undermine the walls" of an enemy force.

Today, you can undermine more than walls. You don´t even have to do any digging! Undermining something means to make it weak, or cause it to fail. To undermine a crime, you stop it.

---

Choose the topic sentence.

◯ **The snakehead fish has slimy scales and can grow up to five feet long.**

◯ **Snakeheads are dangerous fish because they do not have any natural enemies in US lakes and rivers.**

---

Draw a line through the word that does not belong.

The library will hold a sale this weekend to raise funds. Reese will have to go early to get the best ideal selection.

---

**scrawl**

◯ write carefully

◯ write hurriedly

---

Spell the word correctly.

**blaime**

_____

---

**meenwhile**

**meanwhile**

**meanwile**

---

Nathan wore only a T-shirt and shorts. He was

_____.

**underdone     underlined     underdressed**

Circle three antonyms for **bright**.

**dark**     **light**

**smart**     **dim**

**gloomy**     **brilliant**

does anyone here have the time? asked cole it's quarter past two said maggie

_____

_____

_____

Jeanine _____ across the field to catch the baseball in time.

**ran**     **scampered**

Julio _____ into the room like a storm cloud.

○ **walked**

○ **thundered**

○ **skipped**

○ **imitait**

○ **imitaite**

○ **imitate**

   Maxwell's grandfather would not use a computer. He said he liked writing with a pencil better. "You can't hack a pencil," he would laugh. Then, the family got him a special present. It was a new laptop. But, you know what? Maxwell's grandfather still uses a pencil!

Which proverb or adage matches this explanation?

○ **Birds of a feather flock together.**

○ **You can lead a horse to water, but you can't make him drink.**

○ **When in Rome, do as the Romans do.**

**pursuade**

**persuade**

**perswede**

Write a heading for each section of the informational piece.

_____

   Many dogs are trained in K-9 units for police departments. They can help find people who are lost and have even saved people's lives. They work with police officers called "handlers."

_____

   Dogs also herd sheep. Border collies are a popular breed of dog for this type of work. They watch the herd closely to make sure all of the sheep stay together. If a sheep tries to stray, the dog will nip gently at its feet to direct it back to the herd.

_____

   Therapy or service dogs help people with physical and emotional challenges. Because of their training, these dogs are allowed to go anywhere their people go—even the movies! They have saved many lives. Some have called 911 when their owners were ill.

Fill in the blanks with **is**, **am**, or **are**.

I _____ waiting for calls from two friends.

Both of them _____ coming home after weekend

trips. The grass _____ growing under my feet,

as my grandmother says.

Correct the sentence.

They're are to many onions on there

pizza.

Place a dot (•) between syllables.

u n d e r a r m

u n d e r t a k e

u n d e r l y i n g

Circle each word that could be an object to a preposition.

**along**

**floor**

**about**

**threw**

**through**

**barn**

**pony**

○ **settil**

○ **settle**

○ **setle**

Circle the stronger sentence.

Ryan went over soon after.

Ryan sprinted to the house.

Many kids have cell phones today. When is a child too young to have one? Write an opinion about this topic and connect your reasons by using words and phrases such as *for instance*, *in order to*, and *in addition to*.

_____

_____

_____

_____

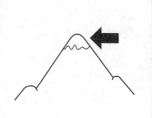

○ **peak**

○ **peek**

**The next night**, Kai stayed up late to practice in his room.

**indirect object**     **transition phrase**

I _____ studying right now.

---

Underline the present tense verb(s).

The new bridge will be opening this weekend. A ribbon-cutting ceremony will be held on Saturday. I am looking forward to it. My brother and I are planning to go. Do you have any plans for the weekend? You are welcome to come with us if you want. We will be looking for spots near the river.

---

row  ➡  **was rowing**

map  ➡  _____

dare ➡  _____

ask  ➡  _____

rake ➡  _____

fool ➡  _____

---

Place a ✓ by each synonym.

**pause**

☐ search

☐ stop

☐ wait

☐ frozen

☐ hold on

☐ rest

---

" _____ Molly and Ian be in the play?"
"I think so. It sounds like they _____ rehearsing their lines."
"When _____ they _____ trying out for the play?"
"Tryouts are _____ held tomorrow."

---

Lily and Meg _____ practice without saying anything.

**leafed      left      leaved**

---

Place a ✓ by each word with the vowel sound in **win**.

☐ **China**

☐ **criminal**

☐ **defend**

☐ **pinning**

☐ **pining**

☐ **signed**

---

Fill in the base words.

➡ ruining  edging  knitting  being

⬇ raking  netting

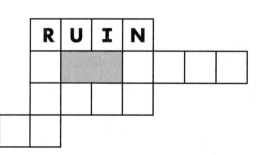

---

**incomplete (n.)**

○ stop completing

○ not complete

○ become complete

---

Frank raked the (leafs, leaves) into

a pile.

That was the (boys´, boys) last chore for

the day.

---

Malcom _____ the ball down the basketball court.

**bounced**     **dribbled**

Ricardo _____ the ball into the hoop.

**dunked**     **threw**

---

You are interviewing the superintendent of schools for the school newspaper. You want to know why the music programs have been cut from the school schedule for the following year. Select the pieces of information that you should use in the article to support your topic.

○ **A.** a quote from the superintendent about budget cuts

○ **B.** a schedule of an upcoming school talent show

○ **C.** a comparison of how much money is spent on music compared to other subjects

○ **D.** a quote from the music teacher about the budget cuts

○ **E.** a list of your favorite singers and songs

---

Fill in the antonyms.

→ rise        ancient

↓ pupil

nervous

|   |   |   |   |
|---|---|---|---|
|   |   |   |   |

| F | A | L | L |

---

He sailed across the room like a

_____.

○ **boat**

○ **truck**

○ **train**

She worked as hard as a

_____.

○ **beaver**

○ **snail**

---

Dear Mrs. Pine,

○ **formal**

○ **informal**

---

Spell the word correctly.

**dairey**

_____

---

○ **nives**

○ **knives**

○ **knifes**

---

over = above

overfly = fly above

overhead = _____

Name _____

Circle two synonyms. Use one in a sentence.

**protect    homestead    safety    defend**

_____

_____

_____

Wear will you be siting at the dinner tonite?

_____

_____

"Shall we dance?"

**informal        informal**

When the game began, the children **scurried** like frightened mice.

Circle the meaning of **scurried**.

**ran quickly**

**ran slowly**

Marcy thought she was going to have a quiet day. Then, **out of the blue**, three of her best friends showed up to surprise her.

What does the idiom mean?

_____

_____

_____

_____

_____

Complete the synonym.

**mood**

f___ ___ling

Write about what you will be doing after you get home from school today.

_____

_____

_____

_____

_____

_____

_____

**overpass (n.)**

◯ road that goes over another

◯ connecting road

Fill in the blanks with forms of **have**.

Kai´s birthday was last week, but he _____

the flu and did not celebrate. To make up for it, he is

_____ a party this Friday. We will _____

a whole bowling alley to ourselves!

---

When I made it to the top of the hill, I had to catch my (breath, breathe). I was (breathing, breatheing) heavily.

---

Place a dot (•) between syllables.

w e a r i n g

n e s t i n g

s t o r i n g

---

Gerry is doing not anything.

What two words should be switched?

_____

_____

---

○ **curios**

○ **curious**

○ **curius**

---

Underline the detail that could be better expressed in a chart or graph.

A local group went from house to house to ask residents what they thought of the new law. A greater number of older residents than younger residents were in favor of the law.

---

Write a concluding statement for the opinion piece.

Many kids in cities live close enough to their schools to walk, but these kids often take a bus or are driven to school by an adult. This means more car pollution and less time for kids to move around before the school day begins.

One solution to this problem is for kids to form a "walking bus." A walking bus is formed when a few parents volunteer to walk a group of kids to school. The volunteers start with the kid who lives farthest away, and they pick up other kids along the way to the school.

_____

_____

---

Laura Roberts
105 Ashe St.
Columbia, SC 29451

Sam Anderson
229 Atlantic Ave.
Atlanta, GA 30135

○ **mail**

○ **male**

---

The construction crew **will** repave the road next month.

**main verb**          **helping verb**

My ancestors came from Greenland,

_____ is actually covered with ice.

Write an informational report about how to play a game. Link your ideas with words and phrases such as *for example*, *also*, and *another*.

_____

_____

_____

_____

_____

Draw lines through the mistakes and correct them.

  Students will studying geology after winter break. We suggest splitting students into pairs for outside activities. When the weather is gooding, they will work on their rock collecktions.

_____

_____

Place a ✓ by each synonym.

**help**

❏ aid

❏ relief

❏ try

❏ assist

❏ work

❏ ask

the blue big house

the piping hot oven

the flying amazing squirrel

the majestic humpback whale

the big blue house

the hot piping oven

the amazing flying squirrel

the humpback majestic whale

Place a ✓ by each antonym.

**help**

❏ make

❏ try

❏ worsen

❏ see

❏ hurt

I (can, may, must) study for the test to pass it.

Sort the correctly and incorrectly spelled words.

**blindefold   gluve   wildernes   maker
lemmon   cover   kettle   robber**

| correct | incorrect |
|---------|-----------|
|         |           |

Excuse me ___ but do

you know which bus

this is___

I'm not sure ___ but I

sure am excited___

They only (began, begun) work on the new house this August.

I (saw, seen) them at work this past weekend.

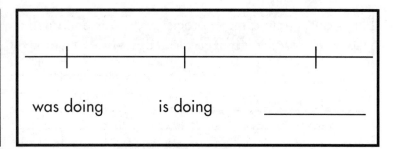

was doing          is doing          _____

What type of food would you like to see served in your school cafeteria? Write an opinion of a food that you want to see on the menu that the school will not presently serve. Give reasons to support your opinion.

_____

_____

_____

_____

_____

_____

_____

Fill in the antonyms.

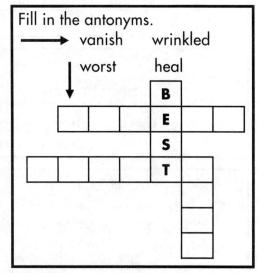

→ vanish     wrinkled

worst     heal

Phillipe, a true _____, liked to study until the wee hours of the morning.

○ **couch potato**

○ **apple pie**

○ **night owl**

What will you be _____ (wear) to the costume party?

Complete the synonym.

**stare**

g___ ___re

○ **scithe**

○ **scythe**

○ **scyth**

oversleep = sleep too much

overeat = eat too much

overdo = _____

Find and circle a more precise word for each item.
**dive (in air), tree stub, leather shoe, squash**

| A | Y | E | L | C | H | P | O |
|---|---|---|---|---|---|---|---|
| L | D | C | B | B | I | U | X |
| N | S | L | S | T | U | M | P |
| Q | W | O | Y | S | W | P | V |
| U | O | F | H | J | R | K | T |
| M | O | C | C | A | S | I | N |
| O | P | R | R | U | T | N | E |

what will you painting for your art assignment

_____

_____

_____

Evan is _____ his pencils.

**sharpning      sharpenning      sharpening**

He heard the crashing of books, which were falling off of his crowded desk like an **avalanche** made of paper instead of snow.

Circle the meaning of **avalanche**.

a huge pile of books falling down

a huge amount of snow falling down

Misha had a great summer at camp. But, now camp was over, and school was about to start. When he unpacked his bags, he flopped down on his bed and realized how soft his bed was. The camp beds were made of wood and were not that comfortable. He smiled, knowing he would get a great night's sleep!

Which proverb or adage sums up this situation?

○ **One man's trash is another man's treasure.**

○ **All good things must come to an end.**

○ **There's no place like home.**

Spell the word correctly.

**tunnell**

_____

Write a heading for each section of the informational piece.

_____

The bald eagle is a magnificent bird. Its rich, brown feathers contrast the bright, white feathers of its head. Its eyes make the eagle look very serious. This bird is the national bird of the United States.

_____

The bald eagle almost went extinct. In the late 1700s, there were over 100,000 nesting pairs of eagles. By the 1960s, there were less than 500. Many birds were killed by hunters, but the biggest threat was a chemical called DDT that affected the eggs of eagles.

_____

In the 1970s, the US government passed laws to protect the bald eagle from being hunted. DDT was also banned. Today, the bald eagle is thriving again.

**overripe**

○ ripened too quickly

○ no longer ripe

○ too ripe

Name _____     **Week 9, Day 1**

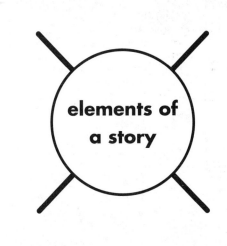

elements of a story

Articles such as **the** and **an** are special types of (adjectives, pronouns).

go ➝ **going**

hurtle ➝ _____

barrel ➝ _____

seal ➝ _____

---

Add prefixes to make new words.

_____ground

_____behave

_____scope

_____possible

_____cycle

---

Complete the synonym.

**shelf**

l__d__e

---

**Overpay** means

_____

_____

_____.

---

What is your school day like? What classes do you take? Do you get a chance to play outside? Write a paragraph that includes information about your school day.

_____

_____

_____

_____

_____

---

We are running always late!

What two words should be switched?

_____

_____

---

Because Jill <u>over</u>slept, she missed breakfast.

**root word**          **prefix**

---

**49**

Circle the prepositional phrases.

An otter slid down a hill into a river by the field.

The old apple tree snatched the balloon from the air with its craggy branches.

What are the branches of the tree acting like?

**eyes**

**fingers**

**feet**

What does "He who hesitates is lost" mean?

_____

_____

_____

_____

Place a ✓ by each synonym.

**hot**

☐ boiling
☐ baking
☐ slipping
☐ sizzling
☐ fiddling
☐ steering

Circle the suffix or prefix in each word.

autograph     disappoint     brightness

telephone     apartment     preview

underfed     creation     nonfat

This really is the house (that, which) Jack built.

Place a ✓ by each antonym.

**hot**

☐ keeping
☐ shiver
☐ scalding
☐ freezing
☐ nippy
☐ chilly

Isaac was shy and often worried about talking with others. He thought he never had anything **relevant** to say. If someone brought up movies, for example, he always felt one step behind. To tell the truth, he hadn't seen a lot of movies.

**Relevant** means _____.

**on topic**     **off topic**

**Miscommunication**

means _____

_____

_____

_____

_____.

(Our, are) new basketball uniforms came in today.

What size (our, are) you?

---

The broken faucet _____ water all over the kitchen.

**poured**     **splattered**

---

Write a heading for each section of the essay on choosing a dog for a pet.

_____

When choosing a puppy from a litter, watch how the puppies interact. Alpha dogs like to be in charge. They can make wonderful pets but may need more training. Shy or nervous puppies will most likely be submissive, which means they are more willing to obey your commands.

_____

At an animal shelter, find out about a dog's history. The shelter workers will be able to tell you about his personality and how he behaves around people, other dogs, and even cats. Most shelters will let you spend time with the dog and even take him on a short walk to see how you interact with each other. If it is a good fit, you may be bringing home the best dog in the world!

---

Fill in the synonyms.

→ warrior
notice (verb)

↓ mop
voyage

|   |   |   | **W** |   |
|---|---|---|---|---|
|   |   |   | **I** |   |
|   |   |   | **P** |   |
|   |   | **E** |   |   |

---

Select the transitional and linking phrases.

○ **in order to**

○ **forever mine**

○ **for instance**

○ **whomever is chosen**

○ **in addition to**

---

Correct the misspelled words.
The old man had a hangkerchief in his pocket. He was smiling and seemed to be in a good mude.

_____  _____

---

○ **royl**

○ **royel**

○ **royal**

---

Betsy's mom pressed a flower

_____ the pages of

a book.

---

Because Lauren _____ herself, she now feels tired.
**overworked     overtop     overheard**
To give herself a break, she decided to _____ the next morning.
**overturn     oversleep     overact**

---

Circle the two synonyms. Use one in a sentence.

**fake    hoax    fix    shuck**

_____

_____

---

botswana angola and zambia are african countries

_____

_____

_____

---

Ethan, _____ I invited to join us today, _____

not _____ coming after all.

---

When Mrs. Morgan looked outside, she was completely **bewildered** by the vast number of paper hearts in her front yard.

Circle the meaning of **bewildered**.

wild about something

confused about something

---

Lindsey did not like the new girl, Marta, because she never spoke and seemed very stuck up. Then one day, Lindsay started talking to Marta on the bus, and Marta was actually very nice. Lindsay realized that Marta was not stuck up at all, just very shy.

Which proverb or adage sums up this situation?

- ⃝ **Good things come to those that wait.**
- ⃝ **Two heads are better than one.**
- ⃝ **Don't judge a book by its cover.**

---

Spell the word correctly.

**beeak**

_____

---

Write an imaginary or real story about an adventure you have had or would like to have. Use sensory words to help the reader visualize your story.

_____

_____

_____

_____

_____

_____

_____

_____

_____

---

**ingineer**

**engineer**

**enginear**

---

Fill in the blanks with punctuation marks.

___What flavor will you get__ __ Berry asked__

___Oh__ I don't know__ __ I said__ ___What

were you thinking of getting__ __

___I always get coconut__ __ Berry replied__

___but it looks like they're fresh out__ It's a

shame__ __

When writing an opinion essay, it is good to know who your (readers, characters) are.

Place a dot (•) between syllables.

o v e r p a s s

o v e r c o o k e d

o v e r h a n g i n g

---

That show uses a lot of **running** jokes.

○ **noun**

○ **verb**

○ **adjective**

Spell the word correctly.

**wheate**

_____

Circle the stronger sentence.

Ella put in the nail.

Ella hammered in the nail.

You are about to write a research paper. List two things you should do below each step.

| plan | write | revise |
|------|-------|--------|
|      |       |        |

○ **poll**

○ **pole**

The four horses grazed on the overgrown grass in the pasture.

**simple sentence**          **compound sentence**

When (can, may, must) I use the computer to do my homework?

---

Max wanted to play cards. Neal wanted to shoot hoops. Because they did not want to disagree, they decided to **see eye to eye** and go hiking instead.

What does the idiom mean? _____

_____

_____

Find and circle three synonyms for **cry**.

| S | N | I | F | T | L | E |
|---|---|---|---|---|---|---|
| Y | W | E | E | P | Q | U |
| A | A | D | O | S | G | E |
| X | I | C | F | O | H | V |
| B | L | U | B | B | E | R |

Circle the prepositions.

**upon**

**sea**

**under**

**meadow**

**above**

**river**

Juan was **as quiet as a mouse**.

How can someone be **as quiet as a mouse**?

_____

_____

Insert the missing comma.

Lavon finished the book and his mother returned it to the library.

Place a ✓ by each word with the vowel sound in **crust**.

☐ **cruises**

☐ **plus**

☐ **overdue**

☐ **refuses**

☐ **posture**

☐ **fusses**

Sort the words into nouns, verbs, and adjectives.

**misdeed   misspell   misbehavior   underwater
underlie   underneath   overstep   overcook**

| nouns | verbs | adjectives |
|---|---|---|
| | | |

Circle the words that can be objects of prepositions.

**sky**

**through**

**cat**

**tree**

**around**

**by**

The players are not (wait, waiting) any longer to start the game.

Mara will (be, be being) upset if she walks in late.

---

The old, warped door _____ as Jared passed through it.

**creaked loudly**

**made a loud squeaking noise**

---

Insert the transition words and phrases from the word bank to complete this information piece.

**Before   Finally   First   For example   Once   Then**

   Making a salad is very easy. _____ you begin, though, you need to decide on which ingredients to use. _____, you can use leafy greens, other vegetables, fruit, nuts, and cheese—even meat. The most important thing is to combine foods that taste good together.
   _____ you have decided what ingredients to use, you are ready to make a salad! _____, you need to clean, peel, and chop your ingredients, if necessary. _____, put all of your ingredients in a bowl with the greens on the bottom and the heavy to lighter ingredients on top. _____, simply toss your salad with some dressing, and you have a delicious meal!

---

Fill in the synonyms.

→ decoration, duty

↓ forest, insist, interrupt

W
O
O
D
S

---

She cried a _____ of tears.

He is my shining _____.

Laughter is the best

_____.

They were two _____ in a pod.

---

**munch**

○ eat quickly

○ chew

---

○ **worst**

○ **werst**

○ **wirst**

---

○ **squawking grey goose**

○ **grey squawking goose**

---

*mis-* = bad or _____

*under-* = too little or _____

*over-* = too much or _____

List three words that you would use in a report about zoos.

_____  _____  _____

List three words that you would use in a report about aquariums.

_____  _____  _____

Circle the cause. Underline the effect.

The food fight incident led to stricter

cafeteria rules.

_____ a game _____ hide-and-seek,

Ezra found Christina _____ the table because she

_____ munching on pretzels.

The football players **butted** each other with their helmets like rams do with their horns.

Circle the meaning of **butted**.

pushed against with heads

locked horns in a fight when pretending to be rams

Joyce and her mother went to the florist to buy a bouquet of flowers for the living room. Joyce ran over to the red roses. They were beautiful! She turned and saw her mother buying a large bunch of daises. "Why can't we get the roses?" Joyce asked. "Because **they cost an arm and a leg**," her mother laughed. "We'll save roses for a special occasion!"

What does the idiom mean?

_____

_____

_____

Complete the synonym.

**creek**

b__ __ __k

Think of an activity you like to do outdoors. What do you have to do to prepare for it?

_____
_____
_____
_____
_____
_____
_____
_____

**misquote**

◯ not quote

◯ quote someone wrongly

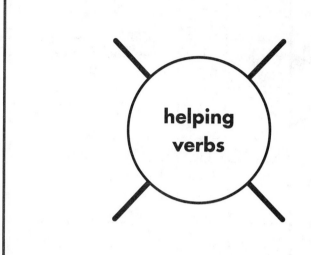

The (conclusion, theme) of a story, poem, or play is its central message.

Write a concluding sentence.

A bald eagle flew over Marco's head to the top of a tree. The eagle was perched on his nest! Marco wanted to learn more about eagles.

_____

_____

Complete the prepositional phrases.

around _____

between _____

through _____

over _____

under _____

above _____

○ **trimed**

○ **trimt**

○ **trimmed**

Add commas and quotations marks.

Good morning Tran Justine said. I hoped to see you in class today. Ms. Sanchez would like us to split up into reading groups and I would like you to be in mine.

You have been assigned to write a research paper about animals that live in the desert. Write a title and three headings you would use in your paper.

Title: _____

Heading 1: _____

Heading 2: _____

Heading 3: _____

I made barely it to the store on time.

What two words should be switched?

_____

_____

The package _____ be coming until Tuesday.

**not          won´t          isn´t**

I can't believe my favorite writer will be reading at the bookstore tonight___

---

When Sara found out her painting was accepted into the art show, her smile **beamed brightly all day long**.

What is Sara's smile like?

○ **the sun**

○ **the moon**

○ **the ocean**

---

Write a conclusion.

Aika heard her name called. She suddenly felt very nervous. She had never participated in a spelling bee before. The announcer paused before calling out the word Aika was to spell. Aika smiled. She knew this word and what it meant. Her father had one under his nose.

_____

_____

---

Place a ✓ by each synonym.

**see**

❑ ocean

❑ spot

❑ search

❑ discern

❑ waters

❑ glimpse

---

At first, Adam felt like **a fish out of water** at the soccer game, but he soon felt welcome when everyone said hello to him.

What does the idiom mean?

_____

---

I can play with you soon, but right now I _____ helping my mom.

---

Place a ✓ by each object pronoun.

❑ her

❑ us

❑ you

❑ he

❑ it

❑ its

❑ them

---

My Uncle Stu is **verbose**. If you ask him how his day is going, he'll talk your ear off. "Oh, I don't mind telling you that I am certainly having a marvelously wonderful day of it all," he might say. "You can be sure of that and make no mistake about it."

**Verbose** means _____ .

**cheery   wordy   organized**

Underline the idiom in the paragraph and describe what it means. _____

_____

---

**Misunderstand** means

_____

_____

_____

_____ .

(To, Too, Two) of my friends went (to, too, two) the city today.

I want to go into the city (to, too, two).

---

The big blue balloon _____ when it flew into a sharp tree branch.

**blew up      popped**

The tree limb _____ when Alex tried to climb it.

**snapped      broke**

---

What is the best exercise that people can do? Give reasons to support your opinion.

_____

_____

_____

_____

_____

_____

_____

_____

_____

---

Rewrite the sentence correctly.

Before michigan was admitted to the united states, It had been a separate Territory for about Thirty Years.

_____

_____

_____

---

_____ the starlit sky

_____ the ocean wide

_____ a wall

_____ the woods

_____ the bend

---

**jabber**

○ talk quietly

○ talk speedily

---

Complete the synonym.

**mix**

___len___

---

**gleme**

**gleam**

**gleem**

---

inactive = not active

impatient = not patient

incomplete = _____

---

Name _____

Circle the two synonyms. Use one in a sentence.

**thrilled**　　**delighted**

**expected**　　**peeled**

_____

_____

---

i was going to ask her but she had already left.

_____

_____

---

Remy, (whom, whose) mom works with my dad, (is, will) running in a 10K race today.

---

Unlike woolen clothes, which often feel very soft, the wool on a sheep feels very **coarse** to the touch. What is the meaning of **coarse**?

_____

_____

---

Elise and her mother planted a vegetable garden. Every day, they watered the plants, but to Elise, it seemed like they were watering dirt instead. One day, Elise saw a few green shoots and then more. Soon the garden was brimming with young plants!

Which proverb or adage sums up his situation?

( ) **A penny saved is a penny earned.**

( ) **Good things come to those who wait.**

( ) **The grass is always greener on the other side of the fence.**

---

Spell the word correctly.

**forgeive**

_____

---

Fill in the blanks with forms of **have**.

"_____ Sophia gotten her medal yet?"

"No. She was _____ a hard time hiding her impatience when it didn't come yesterday."

"I'm _____ dinner with her family tonight. I'll _____ to remember not to bring it up."

"She _____ to work on her patience, though. It's not good to _____ that sort of thing take over your life."

"No, but I _____ trouble with it myself."

---

**imperfect (adj.)**

( ) not perfect

( ) not perfect yet

( ) never perfect

---

Underline the fragments and circle the run-ons.

Many immigrants came to the United States from Europe in the mid-1800s. During the Great Famine, a number of Irish citizens came hoping for prosperity, they were not the only ones coming at the time. Norwegians, Swedes, and Germans also. They mainly moved to the Midwest. Large groups of Norwegian and Swedish immigrants settled in Minnesota and nearby states.

Punctuate the sentence.

What day is the science fair___

Place a dot (•) between syllables.

i m m e d i a t e

i m p r e s s

i m p a t i e n t

Add suffixes to make new words.

excite _____

teach _____

act_____

dark _____

wood _____

Complete the antonym.

**calm**

ex___ ___t___d

Circle the correct word.
I (can, must) remember to bring the tickets to the concert.
I (may, can) walk two miles in one morning.
(Must, May) I borrow a ruler to measure my poster?

**conservation    endangered    extinction
habitat    wildlife**

Use the word bank to fill in the blanks.

When people use forest products to build homes and other buildings,

_____ often loses its natural _____.

Without a place to live, these animals can become

_____. It is up to _____ efforts by people

to protect these creatures from _____.

○ **paws**

○ **pause**

George's family might _____ to the fair.

**come        coming        came**

Yesterday, I _____ riding my bike through the park.

---

You are writing an informational report about how to plant a vegetable garden. Describe two illustrations you would like to include. List two headings you would place in the report.

| illustrations | headings |
|---|---|
|  |  |
|  |  |
|  |  |

---

After winning the race, Michaela felt like she was

_____.

**at the end of her rope**

**out of the fire into the frying pan**

**on top of the world**

---

Place a ✓ by each synonym.

**yell**

☐ loudly

☐ call out

☐ wail

☐ cry

☐ spray

☐ roar

---

Jacqui ____ _____, "We must be quiet, or we will wake up Grandpa from his nap."

**bellowed**

**whispered**

**sneered**

---

I _____ bird watching at a national park tomorrow.

---

Place a ✓ by each helping verb.

☐ **will**

☐ **pull**

☐ **can**

☐ **say**

☐ **might**

☐ **sell**

☐ **without**

---

Write an introduction to an imaginary short story about two characters who live on another planet. Have a narrator tell the story and introduce the characters.

_____

_____

_____

_____

_____

---

_____ many ponies

**to**

**too**

**two**

Name _____

Week 12, Day 3

(Theirs, There's) not enough room for the books.

That bookshelf is (theirs, there's).

---

Bryce does so well in school: the more _____ the test, the _____ it seems to him.

**easier**      **difficult**

---

Write a short story about a character who is climbing a mountain. Describe the action of the story in detail. Link the sentences describing the action with linking words and phrases such as *at first*, *then*, and *finally*.

_____

_____

_____

_____

_____

_____

_____

_____

_____

---

What is the idiom for the word puzzle?

**OVER
MOON**

_____

_____

_____

---

Scott's temper can _____ like a volcano at any moment.

Which word best fits the simile?

◯ **act**

◯ **erupt**

◯ **gurgle**

---

Break up the contractions.
_____ (There's) a small park around the corner that _____ (I've) always enjoyed visiting.

---

Spell the word correctly.

**howul**

_____

---

◯ **waltz**

◯ **walts**

◯ **walltz**

---

disapprove = not approve

disbelieve = not believe

disobey = _____

---

Circle the helping verb. Use it in a sentence.

**maybe    willing    can    meet**

_____

_____

Circle the informal words.

Thanks for your help this weekend. We

loved seeing you guys!

Elsa wore a dress as _____ as rubies

_____ her mother had sewed by hand.

Marcy's oldest sister is **consulting** with her academic advisor because she is not sure what courses to take.

What does **consulting** mean?

_____

_____

Chen was on her way to her aunt's house when it began to rain. Chen got drenched. Then, a car splashed mud all over her new dress, and the wind blew her hair into a thousand directions. She looked like a rag doll! When her aunt opened the door, she smiled and said, "Chen, you look great!"

Which proverb or adage sums up this situation?

○ **Beauty is a beauty does.**

○ **Beauty is only skin deep.**

○ **Beauty is in the eye of the beholder.**

○ gallen

○ gallon

○ gallun

Write a conclusion for the opinion piece.

Cooking your own meals is good for you. If you buy processed foods, which are foods that are precooked in a factory, you are most likely eating food that is very high in salt and sugar. In high quantities, salt and sugar can be bad for your health. Look at the ingredients on the side of the box and also learn to read the nutritional counts. This will help tell you how healthful your meal is. When you cook your own food, you can leave out the sugar and salt or at least minimize how much you use.

_____

_____

_____

_____

**disown**

○ pick up

○ slip up

○ give up

Underline the run-ons and circle the fragments.

Three families lived in the old Bilby house, one lived on each floor. In the attic, crammed in under a slanting roof, the Miller family. The Matuszweskis lived on the second floor and were always welcoming guests. On the ground floor, the Rios family kept mostly to themselves, they spent most weekends out in the state park.

History textbooks give (firsthand, secondhand) accounts of historical events.

Distrust means

○ **not trust**

○ **trust the right person**

○ **try to trust**

Write three different progressive verb tenses for the word *read*.

Past:

_____ _____

Present:

_____ _____

Future:

_____ _____

○ **emprove**

○ **impruve**

○ **improve**

Write a complete sentence from the fragments.

Kushan's family cooking dinner. Samosas, dal, vegetable korma, and rice.

_____

**glide   utter   declare   hustle   review   cram   inspect   bellow   mutter**

| move | speak | study |
|---|---|---|
|  |  |  |

**Thorough, through, throughout, throwback,** and **throttle** are all polysyllabic words.

○ **true**

○ **false**

I can **leave** as early as 8:00 tonight.

**main verb        helping verb**

I _____ helping my grandfather rake leaves right now.

---

The monarch butterfly is orange with black stripes. Like a bee, it can pollinate plants. Every year, it travels from Mexico and across the United States to Canada.

**informative**          **narrative**

**opinion**

---

Read the sentence. Continue the paragraph by stating an opinion.

Some cities are beginning to allow people to raise chickens in their backyards, which is a great way to get fresh eggs!

_____

_____

_____

_____

---

Place a ✓ by each synonym.

**late**

☐ before

☐ dally

☐ overdue

☐ wait

☐ beyond

☐ delayed

---

miss schwartz asked how was your trip to hawaii

---

The news team is _____ the race on camera.

**captouring**          **capturing**

**captiuring**

---

Place a ✓ by each antonym.

**late**

☐ early

☐ after

☐ beyond

☐ hurry

☐ hopeful

☐ too soon

---

Last year, my parents and I visited New York City. We first went to Ellis Island, a station where my father's ancestors entered America. We then visited the Statue of Liberty for my mother, who wanted to climb to the top of it. Then, it was my turn to choose, so we went to Coney Island, an amusement park, and had fun all day!

**informative**

**narrative**

**opinion**

---

Circle the word(s) with a **long e** sound.

The weight lifter was

relieved when the gym

reopened.

---

The twins _____ _____ a room this year.

They _____ _____ in the school play.

**star        share**

○ **That sharp kitchen knife is used to chop vegetables.**

○ **That kitchen sharp knife is used to chop vegetables.**

You are writing an informational piece about an animal shelter for rescued tigers in the United States. Select the best choice for an image to use in your report.

○ **a tiger chasing a deer in the wild**

○ **a tiger roaring in the middle of a jungle**

○ **a tiger lying peacefully under a maple tree**

○ **a tiger jumping through a hoop in a circus ring**

What is the idiom for the word puzzle?

**INlostTHOUGHT**

_____

_____

_____

_____

Circle the words that could be used in a report about train travel.

**tractor**

**caboose**

**rubber tires**

**railroad tracks**

**engine**

**conductor**

is snowing

○ **snows now**

○ **snowed just now**

Complete the synonym.

**cattle**

o___ ___n

○ **reindeer**

○ **raindeer**

○ **reigndeer**

Mr. Brownlee was **displeased** with the badly behaved class.

**not polite        not happy**

List three words that you would use in a report about freshwater fish.

_____

_____

_____

could you drive me there or is it too late

_____

_____

Punctuate the sentence correctly.

Olaf is entering the building now so he will be on time for his class

Owen's dad slapped him on the shoulder and said, "Great job on your report, son. I give you a lot of **credit** for all of the work you did on that."

Circle the meaning of **credit**.

**recognition**

**dismissal**

Carlotta told Matthew that his shirt was inside out. Matthew looked down and saw that it was on right. "**Stop pulling my leg**!" he laughed.

What does the idiom mean?

_____

_____

_____

_____

Spell the word correctly.

**fieerce**

_____

Imagine your first day on your dream job 15 years from now. What is the job? Where is it? Write a dialogue with one of your co-workers.

_____

_____

_____

_____

_____

_____

_____

_____

**polare**

**poelar**

**polar**

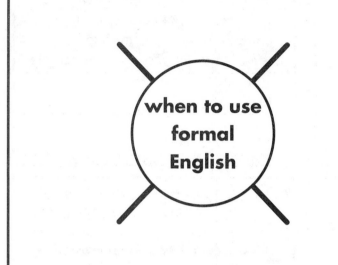

Informational text should use (inference, evidence) to back up its points.

Place a dot (•) between syllables.

t r o u b l e

s q u a b b l e

u n a b l e

Complete the prepositional phrases.

through _____

within _____

across _____

beneath _____

in _____

on _____

Complete the synonym.

**deliver**

___rin___

Add commas and quotations marks.

Hey Tommy Juanita called out. Are you going to enter a project in the science fair this year? Do you need a partner? If so I think I have some good ideas for an experiment.

Write an informative paragraph about traffic safety at your school. Use concrete details to support your main idea.

_____

_____

_____

_____

_____

_____

_____

Spell the words correctly.

hoetell _____

emprove _____

gelus _____

unyun _____

mehdul _____

**Do** you miss living in your old house?

**main verb**        **helping verb**

Tomorrow, I _____ running with my best friend in a 5K fun run.

---

If you deal with a problem right away, it will not become a bigger one.

Which proverb or adage matches this explanation?

○ **Don't look a gift horse in the mouth.**

○ **Look before you leap.**

○ **A stitch in time saves nine.**

---

Sometimes, when you are waiting for a special day to come or an event to happen, it seems like it takes forever. And, the more you anticipate it, the longer it seems to take.

Which proverb or adage sums up this situation?

○ **A watched pot never boils.**

○ **Don't count your chickens before they're hatched.**

○ **You can't teach an old dog new tricks.**

---

Place a ✓ by each synonym.

**stop**

☐ cut short

☐ knock off

☐ tuck away

☐ shut down

☐ end

☐ shrink

---

Circle the prepositions.

**beneath**          **baby**

**before**          **breakfast**

**broken**          **behind**

---

many people have taken Ferries down the

mississippi river.

---

Place a ✓ by each antonym.

**stop**

☐ open

☐ cut out

☐ begin

☐ leave out

☐ initiate

☐ take up

---

Circle the words that would most likely be used in a report about the solar system.

**Pacific Ocean**     **Pluto**     **ornament**

**orbit**     **corral**     **parachute**

**airplane**     **fire engine**     **satellites**

**submarines**     **craters**     **asteroids**

---

_____ be or not

_____ be

**to**

**too**

**two**

When Alex is away for too long, his cat lies down at the foot of the (stairs, stares) and (stairs, stares) at the front door, waiting for him to come home.

---

The school waving flag flapped in the wind.

The waving school flag flapped in the wind.

---

Write a concluding statement to the informational piece.

Some schools are beginning to recycle cafeteria food scraps using worms. Yes, worms! Squirmy, icky, slimy worms are excellent workers. They break down compost, which is made of plant leaves and food scraps. Eventually, the compost turns into humus, a dark, dirt-like matter. Humus can give plants extra nutrients. Schools take the humus and give it to local farmers for their crops.

_____

_____

_____

_____

_____

_____

---

What is the idiom for the word puzzle?

**WEATHER**
**UNDER**

_____

_____

_____

---

During the agility competition,

Caryn's dog leaped _____

a jump, crawled _____ a

tunnel, slid _____ a pole,

and flew _____ the

finish line.

---

Circle the helping verbs.

The parachutists will jump in five minutes. They have planned their jump so that they will swoop into the park just past that pavilion.

---

○ **erge**

○ **irge**

○ **urge**

---

**baby gurgling boy**

**gurgling baby boy**

---

A bicycle has two wheels.

The suffix -ped means "footed."

A biped walks on _____ .

This is a pair of **binoculars**. If **bi-** means two, what do you think **ocular** means?

_____

the peaches were growing soft when we picked them

_____

_____

_____

Correct the sentence.

Hold on I have an important question for you it can't wait

Kaleigh **demonstrated** what a talented artist she was when she displayed her paintings at the school fair.

Circle the meaning of **demonstrated**.

**painted**

**showed**

Circle the words that need to be capitalized.

our class field trip was to mount

rushmore, which is a sculpture

carved on the side of a mountain

of george washington, thomas

jefferson, abraham lincoln, and

theodore roosevelt.

Spell the word correctly.

**coupple**

_____

Circle the words and phrases that link together opinions and reasons. Write a concluding statement for this opinion piece.

  Clotheslines are a hot issue! For decades, people used to hang their clothes on lines to let the sun dry them. Then, the clothes dryer was introduced, and most people stopped using the clothesline. Some communities even banned people from using clotheslines altogether because they did not like the look of them.
  However, there are many reasons to bring the clothesline back. First, the sun and wind makes clothes smell good. The sun is also easier on clothes, so clothes last longer. Most important, clotheslines save people from using electricity or water.

_____

_____

**tomato**

**tomaeto**

**tomatoe**

Fill in the blanks with **when**, **where**, or **why**.

I love to eat at Old Beany's, _____

you order one or two meals for your entire table. I

don't know _____ I like it so much. I

guess it brings everyone together _____

you all have the same meal. And, you don't have to

cook!

---

There are a lot of mosquitoes (when, where) the wind blows out from the mainland.

---

Draw a line through the word that does not belong.

The article said that the law will go

into effect when next year.

---

Circle the three words that give the best description of different ways someone can move.

**skip**

**walk**

**waddle**

**run**

**scamper**

---

○ **misstake**

○ **mistake**

○ **mestake**

---

Correct the run-on sentence.

My family visited Boston last year we saw a baseball game, went to the Museum of Science, and drove to the shore.

---

| also | because | for example | then |

Use the word bank to fill in the blanks. Capitalize if needed.

_____ hummingbirds are so tiny, they can go inside the petals of flowers to eat something called nectar. They _____ pollinate plants just like bees! _____, the pollen of the flower sticks to them when they are inside the flower. _____, the pollen is transferred to the next flower the hummingbird enters.

---

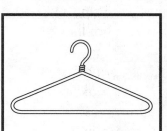

○ **hangar**

○ **hanger**

---

The driver had to go slowly **when** the storm broke.

**relative adverb**     **helping verb**

I (can, may, must) juggle three balls at one time.

---

Circle the correct linking word or phrase.

   (Because, While) George W. Carver did not invent peanut butter, he found over 300 uses for the peanut. (In order to, Another) help farmers, he suggested "crop rotation." (Instead of, Without) planting the same crop each year, they planted peanuts every other year. (Also, Although) this made the soil richer, it left farmers with a lot of peanuts! Carver found many ways to put the peanut to good use.

---

   People should turn off the water when they brush their teeth. They should only use enough water to wet their toothbrushes and then rinse them off. They can fill small cups with water to rinse out their mouths. These simple steps will save gallons of water every day and make it so that water literally does not go down the drain!

**informative**

**narrative**

**opinion**

---

Place a ✓ by each synonym.

**hum**

☐ sing

☐ purr

☐ swing

☐ shriek

☐ clap

☐ buzz

---

"Do you know _____ the banquet will be held?"

"They're hosting it at Brad's. I don't know _____, though."

---

Correct the sentence.

Michael thought the movie was boring but Isabelle enjoyed it.

---

Place a ✓ by each helping verb.

☐ **was**

☐ **up**

☐ **should**

☐ **shall**

☐ **stay**

☐ **to**

☐ **is**

---

Sort the words into verbs and adjectives.

**inactive   improper   impatient   displace**
**distrust   disowned   disagreeable**

| verbs | adjectives |
| --- | --- |
| | |

---

_____ going to the park.

**They're**

**Their**

**There**

Did you see (who, whom) left a set of keys on this desk?

I'll have to find (they, them).

---

Darnell heard wind musical chimes tinkling from next door.

Darnell heard musical wind chimes tinkling from next door.

---

Think about which adage you support: "Look before you leap," or "He who hesitates is lost." Explain the meaning of each adage in your answer. Remember to support your opinion with facts and details.

_____

_____

_____

_____

_____

_____

_____

---

What is the idiom for the word puzzle?

**LOluckyVE**

_____

_____

_____

---

Write a sentence using **where**.

_____

_____

_____

_____

_____

_____

_____

---

Write two adverbs that are **not** relative.

_____

_____

---

Spell the word correctly.

**gasze**

_____

---

where would you find arkansas on a map of the united states

---

A tricycle has three wheels.

A triangle has three angles.

If something is tricolor, it has _____.

**Tripods** are used to keep cameras steady. If **tri-** means three, what do you think **-pod** means?

_____

Circle the helping verbs. Underline the main verbs.

I can meet you there, but I will be running late.

You should wait for me so that we can work on the report.

Margaret studied her notes and said I think I need to do more research on my topic I need more facts to support my ideas.

Leon's class was learning about Henry Puyi, the last **emperor** of China.

Circle the meaning of **emperor**.

**a royal leader**

**a leader just in China**

Frank could not believe his ears! He was going to the play-offs with his dad. "Are you sure he got tickets?" Frank asked his mom. "Yes," she smiled. **"I heard it from the horse's mouth."**

What does the idiom mean?

_____

_____

_____

_____

_____

Complete the antonym.

**war**

p___ ___c___

Write the first paragraph of a story about a young child. Use at least **two** relative adverbs such as *where, when,* or *why.*

_____

_____

_____

_____

_____

_____

_____

_____

**hurrahcane**

**hurrycane**

**hurricane**

Fill in each blank with a relative adverb.

I'd like to find out _____ the Thomas family went away.

I'd like to find out _____ the Thomas family went away.

I'd like to find out _____ the Thomas family went.

How does each choice of relative adverb affect the meaning of the sentence?

_____

_____

_____

---

Use the helping verb **can** to ask whether you are (able, allowed) to do something.

---

Place a dot (•) between syllables.

c a r e l e s s

b l a m e l e s s

f e a r l e s s

---

Ava looked to see it where stopped.

What two words should be switched?

_____

_____

---

Spell the word correctly.

**diarey**

_____

---

Circle the stronger sentence.

**Katie got a dog.**

**Katie got a cute puppy.**

---

Write a short story that occurs in an imaginary world. What happens to you in the story? Do you have an adventure? Describe this world in detail so that the reader can visualize it.

_____

_____

_____

_____

_____

_____

_____

---

○ **throne**

○ **thrown**

---

From nine until two, Baker **helped** his friends at the food court.

**simple past**          **past progressive**

In order to pass my math test, I (can, may, must) study very hard.

Circle the relative adverbs.

The first time we saw Caleb, he was walking with a notebook in his hand. We were curious about why he was carrying it. Every now and then, he would hunch over to write something on a new page. He stopped writing immediately when he saw us. We felt embarrassed to be caught staring at him and quickly walked up to say hello.

Last Saturday, my uncle took me horseback riding. I was very nervous at first, but he let me ride a gentle, old mare named Daisy. I learned how to hold the reins and sit the right way in a saddle. We rode through the woods on a flat trail. By the end of the day, I felt like a real cowgirl!

**informative**

**narrative**

**opinion**

Place a ✓ by each synonym.

**ill**

☐ unwell
☐ asleep
☐ bedridden
☐ sore
☐ homesick
☐ sick

The idiom "Let sleeping dogs lie" means

○ **to be considerate of others.**
○ **to not stir up trouble.**
○ **to allow animals their naps.**

Adding ending punctuation.

When do you take your next violin

lesson____

Place a ✓ by each antonym.

**ill**

☐ weak
☐ out
☐ healthy
☐ well
☐ calm
☐ proud

Write a concluding statement.

Some American Indian tribes used a system of growing crops in which each plant supported another. The most famous of these plant combinations is "The Three Sisters": corn, beans, and squash. The stalk of corn allowed the vine of the beans to grow tall so that the beans could soak in the sun. The sun allowed the beans to process nutrients that nourished the ground for all three plants. In turn, the broad leaves of the squash plants protected the roots of all three plants from the heat of the sun.

_____

_____

Miko said he would wait

over _____.

**their**

**there**

**they're**

© Carson-Dellosa • CD-104878

The florist was wondering (why, when) no one was coming to his shop, (why, when) he saw that his "CLOSED" sign was facing the street!

○ **Rosario is interested in learning about different saltwater fish.**

○ **Rosario is interested in learning about saltwater different fish.**

Mandy was trying not to cry. Everyone was mad at her! It started when her best friend, Shoshana, told her a secret. Mandy had promised never to tell anyone, but during lunch, she couldn't resist telling her other friend Freida the secret as well. Then, Freida told a few other classmates, and they told their friends. By the next day, everyone knew Shoshana's secret! Now, Shoshana won't talk to her. Mandy told Freida and her friends it was their fault for not keeping the secret. Freida and her friends blamed Mandy for telling it in the first place, and everyone started arguing.

"You've really opened up a **Pandora's box** by telling the secret in the first place," Mandy's mother told her that night. "You have a lot of apologizing to do!"

What does Mandy's mother mean by a **Pandora's box** in the context of the story?

_____

_____

What is the idiom for the word puzzle?

**THEinLINES**

_____

_____

_____

Enrico is **sleeping like a log**.

Explain the simile.

_____

_____

_____

_____

Fill in the blank with a relative adverb.
If you read about events in **chronological order**, they have been sorted by
_____ they happened.

Complete the antonym.

**bound**

___r ___e

Later today, I _____

doing my homework.

A quadruped has four feet.

A square is a quadrilateral.

Quadrilaterals have _____ sides.

If you **triple** in height, you grow three times your size. If you **quadruple** in height, you grow _____ times your size.

Rewrite the sentence correctly.

marta said that it would hail but it never did

_____

_____

the lincoln memorial is one of the most popular monuments in washington dc, perhaps _____ lincoln himself was such a popular president.

After a week of taking tests and writing reports, Nancy felt completely **frazzled** and looked forward to a relaxing weekend.

Circle the meaning of **frazzled**.

**relaxed**

**stressed and tired**

Kyle wasn't sure what to do. Naomi wanted to go bicycle riding with him, and Jamal wanted to practice soccer plays with him. **"Stop sitting on the fence,"** his mother said. "It is a beautiful day, and you should be out there!"

What does the idiom mean?

_____

_____

_____

_____

_____

○ **island**

○ **iland**

○ **eiland**

If you could go back in history, what time period would you want to live in, and where would you like to be? Write about your experience in a different time and place. Describe your situation and the people you live, play, or work with. Use sensory details in your story.

__ _____

_____

_____

_____

_____

_____

_____

_____

Circle the prepositions.

**over**

**ru**

**behind**

**jog**

**around**

Circle the correct suffix to complete the underlined word part in each sentence.

Owen asked his teach(-er, -al) to tell the class about her summer vacation.

Marni was filled with happi(-ment, -ness) from playing with her friends all day.

Hannah received a great deal of atten(-tion, -or) for her piano solo.

---

You can use adverbs to give the reader more information about (nouns, verbs).

---

Place a dot (•) between syllables.

f r i g h t e n s

h a p p e n s

i n t e n s e

---

These two sentences mean the same thing.

I liked the motel **where** we stayed.

I liked the motel **at which** we stayed.

○ **true**

○ **false**

---

○ **electric**

○ **elecktric**

○ **electrick**

---

Add commas and quotations marks.

Valerie called out to her best friend Wait up!
What is it? Rebekah asked.
You have been elected class president Valerie answered.

---

Write a short story that has two characters in it. Who are these characters? What happens to them? Make sure the order of action in your story makes sense to the reader.

_____

_____

_____

_____

_____

_____

---

Choose a sport to write an informative report about. List five sports words you will use.

_____

_____

_____

_____

---

**For example**, Benjamin Franklin's son William was loyal to the crown.

**indirect object**          **linking phrase**

Circle the prepositional phrases in the sentence.
The figure skater skated in circles around the ice rink all evening long.

---

Planting grass requires good soil, lots of watering, and time. First, dig up the ground. If the soil is poor in nutrients, add fertilizer into the ground. Then, mix in grass seeds. You will need to water the ground for at least two weeks before you see small green shoots coming out of the ground.

**informative**          **narrative**

**opinion**

---

Write a conversation between two friends who disagree about something. Punctuate the dialogue correctly.

_____

_____

_____

_____

_____

---

Place a ✓ by each synonym.

**rain**

☐ drizzle

☐ shower

☐ wet

☐ drenched

☐ cloudburst

☐ poured

---

Paolo _____ going to the state fair yesterday.

Paolo _____ going to the state fair tomorrow.

Paolo _____ going to the state fair today.

---

Adding ending punctuation.

Wait ____ I will join you in a minute.

---

Place a ✓ by each relative pronoun.

☐ **which**

☐ **who**

☐ **will**

☐ **we**

☐ **with**

☐ **whose**

---

Write a conclusion for the story.

Lucy and Fiona visited their grandmother, who had just moved to a cottage near the ocean. The girls had never been to the ocean before, and they did not know what to expect. Their grandmother packed a picnic lunch for all three of them. They walked down to the beach and spread out a blanket to lay their food on. Suddenly, a seagull landed on the blanket!

_____

_____

---

_____ dog has a red collar.

**Their**

**There**

**They're**

Riley went (when, quietly) to the back of the room (when, quietly) her pencil broke. She sharpened it (quick, quickly).

---

garage          white

Terrance opened the _____ _____ door.

---

Renee was told she had to clean her room, or she could not go swimming with her friends at the community center. She looked at her room and released a heavy sigh. Pieces of games were scattered everywhere. Homework papers littered the floor. Books had tumbled from the shelves onto piles of clothes. How was she going to clean this all in the next hour? Her friends would be leaving for the community center soon, and she wanted to join them.

"I know it seems like you have a **Herculean task** ahead of you," her mother said. "But, once you get started, it won't be as bad as it seems now."

What does **Herculean task** mean in the context of the story?

_____

_____

_____

---

What is the idiom for the word puzzle?

**DON'T CRY**
**SPILT MILK**

_____

_____

_____

---

there    their    they're

Marlan, Geoff, and Anya

said _____ going to

stop by the soccer field on the

way to _____ classes

so that they can see who is

_____ today.

---

**pivot**

◯ turn suddenly

◯ make a wide turn

---

Complete the synonym.

**morsel**

___ru___b

---

Next Tuesday, I _____

starting guitar lessons.

---

nonmember = not a member

nonfat = without fat

nonending = _____

---

Name _____

One blank is missing the word **when**. Fill it in and leave the others blank.

Anjali was playing field hockey _____ yesterday afternoon. It was her first time on the field since _____ she was injured last spring. She was elated _____ she scored her first goal.

Rewrite the sentence correctly.

hector is wonder were to put the goalposts.

_____

_____

thomas nast was a famous cartoonist _____ drawings once helped capture a thief.

Darlene's little brother **hovered** over her so closely that she felt like he was her shadow.

Circle the meaning of **hovered**.

**acted like a shadow**

**stood close by**

Burton's uncle was always kidding him. One time, his uncle told him that a leprechaun had hidden a pot of gold in the backyard. Burton dug holes all day until his mother saw what was happening. "Burton," she sighed, taking the shovel away. "You know you always have to take what your uncle says **with a grain of salt**."

What does the idiom mean?

_____

_____

_____

Spell the word correctly.

**schift**

_____

When writing an opinion piece, when should you first express your opinion? Why?

__ _____

__ _____

Write t_____raph of your opinion on the topic of how n_____en should be allowed to watch each week.

_____

_____

_____

_____

_____

_____

_____

**nonsense**

◯ words that make no sense

◯ words that make sense

When (shall, should) we repair the broken wheel?

How (would, will) I know what your sister looks like?

We (could, ought) to get to the movie on time.

He (may, might) find the cat behind the door.

Why (must, might) I do homework every night?

I (should, could) always do it later.

---

A suffix is placed at the (beginning, end) of a word.

---

Circle the best linking words.

Jeremy wanted to eat more vegetables (because, although) he liked how colorful they are. He did not know (whose, that) vegetables are also very healthful to eat. (For example, However,) kale and spinach are good for your eyes.

---

Circle the three words that best describe ways people speak.

**talk**

**grumble**

**shout**

**mutter**

**whisper**

---

○ **behaven**

○ **behaved**

○ **behad**

---

Place a comma before each coordinating conjunction.

My father did not drive his car, nor did he take the bus to work today.

He wanted to get more exercise, for he felt he was feeling restless.

---

Write a story with two characters who have a problem. What is the problem, and how do they solve it? Write the dialogue between the two characters discussing the situation.

_____

_____

_____

_____

_____

_____

---

○ **vain**

○ **vane**

---

Morris was _____. He thought highly of himself.

**vain**          **vane**

Circle the prepositional phrases.

My uncle lives on a farm by a beautiful mountain in the country.

Circle the similes.

Amelia felt as light as a feather. Her grandmother had just arrived for a visit. She told Amelia that she was as pretty as a picture. Amelia was happy as a clam!

Threading a needle takes concentration. First, you choose a needle that is the right size for the material you will be sewing. Then, you choose a thread that has a color similar to your fabric. Cut the end of the thread, so it is not frayed. Then, slowly push the thread into the eye, or hole, of the needle. Pull the thread through so that it will not slip out of the hole.

**informative      narrative      opinion**

Place a ✓ by each synonym.

**fly**

☐ air

☐ pad

☐ hike

☐ soar

☐ land

☐ glide

Rewrite as one complete sentence.

Mother packing a picnic basket. Salad, sandwiches, fruit, and water.

_____

_____

class mr hopper said  I would like you to write a report about dr martin luther king  jr who was a great leader

Place a ✓ by each word with the vowel sound in **fly**.

☐ **cider**

☐ **skylight**

☐ **partly**

☐ **winking**

☐ **which**

☐ **confide**

Write a story in which you are an animal. Introduce other characters who are animals. Create a problem to solve. Order the events of the story.

_____

_____

_____

_____

She will _____ a jumpsuit today.

**wear**

**where**

**ware**

The picnic will start (when, unless) the game is over.

Abby won't go (when, unless) Ana is coming.

---

Although I _____ _____ studying for most of this evening, I _____ taking a break right now.

---

The inviting smell of freshly baked chocolate cookies pulled Josh into the kitchen. His dad was baking cookies to sell for a school fund-raiser. Josh had been told earlier that he could not have any of these cookies, but when he saw them cooling on the table, he imagined the combination of buttery crumbs and rich chocolate melting in his mouth. When his dad stepped out of the kitchen, Josh snuck a cookie and held it to his mouth.

"Josh!" He jumped when he heard his dad say his name. "What are you doing?

"I could not help it," Josh said with a full mouth. "Your homemade chocolate chip cookies are my **Achilles' heel**."

What does Josh mean by **Achilles' heel**? Explain.

_____

_____

_____

---

Find and circle four words for **how people feel**.

| Q | U | I | C | D | E | E |
|---|---|---|---|---|---|---|
| H | C | O | H | Y | P | A |
| L | C | X | E | D | R | N |
| B | O | R | E | D | L | X |
| E | W | I | R | K | M | I |
| X | Z | R | F | O | T | O |
| A | T | P | U | L | V | U |
| J | E | A | L | O | U | S |

---

Rewrite the sentence correctly.

quentin exclaimed I couldn't believe how spectacular the grand canyon is have you ever been there

_____

_____

_____

_____

---

Circle the helping verbs.

Eduardo had a question about the homework. Could he write his answers on a separate sheet of paper? He thought it would be easier for him.

---

Spell the word correctly.

**ralley**

_____

---

**necessery**

**necessary**

**nesessary**

---

baker = someone who bakes

collector = someone who collects

writer = _____

**Name** _____     **Week 18, Day 4**

Circle the relative pronoun. Use it in a sentence.

**why    when    whose    where**

_____

_____

_____

---

Rewrite the sentence.

mr dalliard who lives next door jogs and sings each morning

_____

_____

---

I _____ going to the concert early so that I _____ get a good seat.

---

Brianna stood backstage for a few minutes to get a **glimpse** of theater life.

What is the meaning of **glimpse**?

_____

_____

_____

---

Howard's dad said he would help him put together his model airplane set. "Do you think it will be hard?" Howard asked. "Not at all," his dad smiled. "**It will be a piece of cake.**"

What does the idiom mean?

_____

_____

_____

_____

_____

---

Complete the synonym.

**warning**

__ l __ r __ __

---

Write a conversation between someone teaching another person how to do or make something. Punctuate the dialogue correctly with commas, periods, and quotation marks.

_____

_____

_____

_____

_____

_____

_____

---

An inspector

○ **is looked at.**

○ **looks for clues.**

○ **cannot see.**

**88**     © Carson-Dellosa • CD-104878

Underline the words that need to be capitalized. Circle the words that should not be capitalized.

My Friend martin is from germany. martin can speak three different Languages: english, german, and spanish. I am going to his house Today. He is going to Teach me how to count to Ten in german.

A relative adverb adds to the meaning of a (noun phrase, contraction).

Place a dot (•) between syllables.

w r i t e r

c i d e r

h a p p i e r

I can't believe I woke up so late___

○ .

○ !

○ ?

Complete the antonym.

**conserve**

___ ___ ___te

Add commas and quotations marks.

Dr. Wilson asked Where do you think Skip hurt himself Amber

On his paw Amber answered. Skip tripped while running. Will he be OK

He will be fine with rest Dr. Wilson said.

Write a paragraph about building something. Use transitional phrases such as *before*, *first*, *then*, and *finally*.

_____

_____

_____

_____

_____

_____

Spell the words correctly.

cupbored

_____

fone

_____

releaf

_____

_____ you need any help with the assignment?

**Should        Do        Have**

Circle the words that are misspelled.

I use the dictionery to learn how to spell mispelled words and to learn what each word meens.

---

Binh worked odd jobs to save for a new bicycle. Other people were hoping to get odd jobs too. Binh decided to start right after breakfast to ask the neighbors if there were any chores he could do for them. Mr. Horowitz told him he needed someone to weed his garden. Binh got the job!

◯ **Look before you leap.**

◯ **Don't put all your eggs in one basket.**

◯ **The early bird gets the worm.**

---

Did you know you can attract hummingbirds by planting certain types of flowers? Hummingbirds are attracted to flowers with long petals that are shaped like a trumpet. You do not even need a garden—a window box will do!

**informative**

**narrative**

**opinion**

---

Place a ✓ by each word with the vowel sound in **room**.

☐ **prune**

☐ **lunched**

☐ **plodding**

☐ **stunning**

☐ **truthful**

☐ **tuning**

---

Maizie was **fishing for trouble** when she called Bruce a bad name.

**metaphor**

**simile**

---

I (ought, might) to practice the piano every morning to improve my playing.

---

Place a ✓ by each adjective.

☐ **tried**

☐ **tired**

☐ **solid**

☐ **sold**

☐ **merry**

☐ **merrily**

---

Sort the phrases into metaphors and similes.

**gentle as a lamb**
**mirroring her actions**
**swift as a deer**

**drowning in tears**
**hungry as a horse**
**a walking dictionary**

| metaphors | similes |
| --- | --- |
| | |

---

_____ did you put the dog food?

**Wear**

**Where**

**Ware**

When (can, would) Michael meet us for

practice?

He (can, is) joining us at noon.

---

Gina adopted a border young collie from the
animal shelter.

Gina adopted a young border collie from the
animal shelter.

---

Is it ever OK to cheat? If you let a friend copy answers
from a test or homework, is that cheating as well? Write
an opinion piece about cheating and provide reasons
to support your opinion. Link your ideas with words and
phrases such as *for example*, *for instance*, and *because*.

_____

_____

_____

_____

_____

_____

_____

_____

---

Find and circle four words that
mean **to bend your body**.

| C | R | O | U | C | H | R | N |
|---|---|---|---|---|---|---|---|
| J | I | K | S | L | U | M | P |
| O | N | R | Q | G | N | C | Z |
| H | D | P | U | W | C | Y | H |
| K | C | Q | A | V | H | B | P |
| B | E | M | T | E | X | A | T |

---

Angela's voice was music to
his ears.

Explain the metaphor.

_____

_____

_____

_____

_____

---

**cherish**

___ to let go

___ to treasure dearly

---

⃝ **whoose**

⃝ **whouse**

⃝ **whose**

---

I (should, shall, will) now play my

favorite song on the trombone.

---

A diarist keeps a diary.

A flutist plays the flute.

A pianist _____.

---

Circle the two synonyms. Use one in a sentence.

**case    treasure    seek    cherish**

_____

_____

---

Rewrite the sentence correctly.

the sun shone through the curtains, the birds burst into song

_____

_____

---

The ground _____ from the passing of a nearby train.

**shook        rumbled**

---

Stuart read about the **inhabitants** of the cliff villages, prehistoric people who once lived in the southwestern United States.

**Inhabitants** are people

**who live somewhere for a long time.**

**who lived in prehistoric times in the southwest**.

---

Until the 1700s, people who worked with teeth were called **tooth drawers**, because they often had to pull, or draw, teeth. The word **dentist** sounds much nicer. It comes from *dentem*, a Latin word also meaning _____. A dentist is someone who _____ _____.

---

Spell the word correctly.

**onioun**

_____

---

crops   deforestation   habitat   pollinate
pollinators   pesticides   population

   Bees are in big trouble! And, that means trouble for humans as well. Bees _____, or transfer pollen, from one plant to another. Pollen is a powdery substance that helps plants make seeds that then grow into new plants. Although nature has other _____, such as hummingbirds, bees pollinate most of the _____ in America.
   Without bees, we would have very little food to eat. In the last 60 years, the bee _____ (or number of bees) has dropped in the United States from 6 million to 2.5 million! Reasons for this include the loss of their natural _____ (or home) because of _____ (the chopping down of trees and forests) and use of _____ to kill insects that damage crops. Today, the US government is working hard to help bees. So, if you see a bee, don't swat it!

---

**aukward**

**ahkward**

**awkward**

Name _____  Week 20, Day 1

Place a comma before the conjunction that links the two main ideas of each sentence.

Tran and Marco wrote a song and Caryn sang it in front of everyone.

Jennifer thought she left her book at home but it was in her school desk.

Randolph practiced throwing a baseball so now he is ready for the game.

Punctuate the sentence.

Mr. Ito my teacher said  Class you are an amazing group of students

Circle the words that could be used in a report about farm life.

**cows          race car          crops**

**hamsters      chickens      library**

**tractor      guinea pigs      horses**

Circle the words that should be capitalized.

**mr. wang**

**science teacher**

**north pole**

**south america**

**mount everest**

○ **dragen**

○ **dragon**

○ **dragun**

Place a comma before each coordinating conjunction.

I thought I would have pizza for dinner but I ate salad instead.

My friend wants to be a pilot someday so he reads books about airplanes.

Write a brief informative report about making a sculpture. What will you make the sculpture out of? What do you want the sculpture to look like? How will the materials feel in your hands? Use details to help the reader visualize your creation.

_____
_____
_____
_____
_____

Spell the words correctly.

graid _____

grumbull _____

dezine _____

icee _____

glo _____

Her cold was **troublesome**. It would not go away.

**verb          adjective**

© Carson-Dellosa • CD-104878          93

Miko wanted to learn how to play piano _____ he asked his mother if he could take lessons.

---

Planting a young tree involves three basic steps. First, you should remove the burlap sack that covers the root ball. The root ball is just that: a sphere-shaped mass of roots. Plant the tree so that the root ball is almost level with the surface of the ground. Then, add soil and water daily for the next few weeks.

**informative        narrative**

**opinion**

---

What does the adage "The night has a thousand eyes" mean?

**There are a great number of stars in the sky.**

**Be careful of your actions, because someone will usually see you.**

**It can be hard to sleep with so much light.**

---

Place a ✓ by each synonym.

**lead**

❏ guide

❏ back

❏ listen

❏ head

❏ steer

❏ talk

---

I just had a great conversation with my uncle, (who, whom) I admire very much.

---

_____ Marta wanted to sing in the school play, she practiced very hard.

---

Place a ✓ by each antonym.

**lead**

❏ know

❏ trail

❏ speak

❏ go behind

❏ read

❏ follow

---

What qualities make someone a good teacher. Give reasons to support your opinion.

_____

_____

_____

_____

_____

_____

---

The tidy cat groomed _____ fur.

**its**

**it's**

Sidney (might, shall) be able to help us with the poster.

When (could, would) you be able to join us for lunch?

I (shall, ought) to go home and help my family make dinner tonight.

---

did you hear that justin sprained his ankle yesterday so he will not be able to run in the next track meet allen asked mr barnett his gym teacher

_____

_____

---

Write an imaginary story about a group of people who need to cross a river. They must build a bridge themselves. What materials do they need? What tools do they have? How do they build the bridge? Use linking words and phrases such as *first*, *second*, and *finally*.

_____

_____

_____

_____

_____

_____

_____

---

Find and circle four words for a **type of sound**.

| Q | U | I | H | S | Y | T |
|---|---|---|---|---|---|---|
| G | H | X | O | M | C | D |
| L | J | I | N | G | L | E |
| P | R | V | K | W | V | C |
| S | C | R | E | E | C | H |
| A | L | K | S | O | N | O |

---

A person should be careful to watch his step or next move to avoid trouble.

Which proverb or adage sums up this situation?

○ **Look before you leap.**

○ **What goes around comes around.**

○ **All that glitters is not gold.**

---

Fill in the blanks with synonyms.

We _____ (looked at)

the map closely before we finally

_____ (took off).

---

Complete the synonym.

**hideout**

l __ i __ __

---

Insert the correct punctuation.

Horses, cows, and sheep____ your

aunt's farm has it all____

---

The turtle _____ up the steep sand dune.

**climbed**

**struggled**

List three words that you would use in a report about computers.

_____

_____

_____

Rewrite the sentence correctly.

how on earth did you find them said carter

_____

_____

The cat _____ on the ledge and then _____ on the mouse down below.

**stood    crouched    pounced    jumped**

The **operator** of the forklift moved several loads of material before taking a break.

Circle the meaning of **operator**.

**someone who controls a machine**

**someone who takes a break**

Vanessa was nervous about teaming up with her cousin, Paula, to play charades. "What if she doesn't understand my moves," Vanessa said. "Don't worry," her mom replied. "Your cousin Paula is pretty much **on the ball**."

What does the idiom mean?

_____

_____

_____

_____

_____

Spell the word correctly.

**remaine**

_____

| hatter    islander    lawyer    reader    southerner |

The suffix -er has a number of meanings. Often, we use it to show what job a person has. Long ago, you would go to a _____ to have your hat mended. You might talk to a _____ if you have to go to court. The suffix -er can also tell us someone's hobby, as any _____ knows. Sometimes -er describes where people are from. A person who lives in the south may be considered a _____, while someone from Hawaii may be called an _____.

**brownie**

**browny**

**brownee**

Use the dash, question mark, or exclamation mark correctly.

I left my homework on the dining room table ____

Are you going to try out for the school play ____

His name was Jack ____ no, it was George.

Circle the correct word.

Miss Perez, (who, that) is my neighbor, grows roses.

Place a dot (•) between syllables.

s t o r y

n a r r a t i v e

d r a m a

Jamie **threw** the ball to Carmen.

Write three other descriptive words or phrases for **threw**.

_____

_____

_____

Spell the word correctly.

**accusse**

_____

Circle the words that should be capitalized.

   Jose's granddad took him to washington, dc. He wanted Jose to see the lincoln memorial and the washington monument. Later, they visited the white house where the president of the united states lives.

When Carmen received the award for good citizenship, her face beamed **as brightly as the sun**.

What does **as brightly as the sun** mean in the sentence? Why might Carmen's face beam **as brightly as the sun**? Explain.

_____

_____

_____

_____

○ **creak**

○ **creek**

Do you have any idea _____ will win?

**who          whom          whose**

My grandmother came from Italy, _____ some people grow olive trees in their backyards!

Circle the prepositional phrases.

The rabbit slipped under the gate and into the backyard. Then, it saw an old dog sleeping on the grass. Startled, the rabbit flew across the ground and squeezed between a fence post and the gate. The dog rolled on its side and snoozed some more.

Sort the phrases into the correct columns

**whiter than snow**
**cold as ice**
**floating on air**

**proud as a peacock**
**fit as a fiddle**
**hotter than an oven**

| metaphors | similes |
|---|---|
|  |  |

Place a ✓ by each synonym.

**story**

☐ floor

☐ narrative

☐ teller

☐ act

☐ lesson

☐ tale

The old gray mare still is not what she used to be.

The gray old mare is still not what she used to be.

I (should, shall) be able to juggle three balls in the air.

Place a ✓ by each type of literature.

☐ **author**

☐ **narrative**

☐ **poem**

☐ **play**

☐ **character**

☐ **chapter**

In the fable "The Grasshopper and the Ant," the ant works all summer long to grow enough food for the winter, while the grasshopper plays in the sun. When winter comes, the hungry grasshopper comes to the ant for help. Write a conversation between the ant and the grasshopper about this situation.

_____

_____

_____

_____

_____ time to go to sleep.

**Its**

**It's**

I am (meating, meeting) Connor this afternoon.

Poultry and fish are both (meats, meets).

---

Confused, Kate _____ her nose and _____ her head.

**wrinkled  moved        touched  scratched**

---

You are writing an informational report about the signing of the US Constitution. Which facts should you include in your report to support the topic?

○ **A.** the list of colonial states that joined the Union

○ **B.** the names of the generals who fought in the American Revolution

○ **C.** a description the USS *Constitution*, a US Navy ship named by George Washington

○ **D.** a summary of the contents of the US Constitution

○ **E.** a description of the Boston Tea Party

---

Find and circle four words for **jerking motion**.

| I | G | H | J | O | M |
|---|---|---|---|---|---|
| S | Q | U | I | R | M |
| T | D | D | U | Y | O |
| W | I | G | G | L | E |
| I | N | M | L | R | P |
| S | A | J | E | K | O |
| T | U | X | I | Z | A |

---

Mr. Benson **chugged** through the hall until he came to a **screeching** halt.

What does the metaphor relate to?

○ **an airplane**

○ **a car**

○ **a train**

---

Write a two-syllable adjective with the same vowel sound as **bought**.

---

○ **arrea**

○ **area**

○ **airea**

---

The rock climber clambered

_____ the mountainside,

_____ was over 1,500 feet.

---

edible = can be eaten

visible = can be seen

fixable = _____

another problem chen sighed is that we do not have enough teammates and we need at least two more people to play against the west somerset wildcats.

Circle the subjects.

Paul left the box on the table, but Brooke soon put it away where it belonged.

After the basketball _____ off the edge of the hoop, the players _____ to catch it.

**bounced      shot      tried      scrambled**

Mrs. Harmon was thrilled that her pet store made a **profit** after the big sale.

Circle the meaning of **profit**.

**a surplus of money**

**a big sale**

Aiden's class was studying the Great Chicago Fire of 1871. When his teacher asked Aiden to explain a major reason for the fire spreading so quickly, he replied, "Because much of the city was made out of wood, including the streets and sidewalks." "You certainly **hit the nail on the head**," his teacher said.

What does the idiom mean?

_____

_____

_____

Complete the antonym.

**hollow**

__ o __ i __

Write a heading for each section of the informational piece on sharks.

_____

How much do you know about sharks? Did you know sharks have no bones? Their bodies are made of cartilage instead, like the material in your nose.

_____

Sharks have excellent eyesight, particularly at night. They are attracted to bright colors such as orange and yellow. Wear dark colors to swim in the ocean!

_____

Sharks can go several weeks without eating. They do not get hungry every day like people do. They eat both meat and vegetables. They will eat just about anything—even license plates and car tires!

**movable**

◯ should be moved

◯ can be moved

◯ might be moved

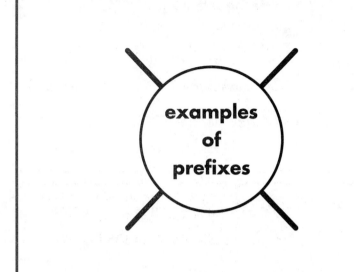

examples
of
prefixes

When you fix spelling and other mistakes in a story, you are (editing, rewriting) the story.

**Doable** means

_____

_____

_____.

Gavin **sat down** on the gym mat.

Write three other descriptive words or phrases for **sat down**.

_____

_____

_____

Complete the synonym.

**incline**

s___o___ ___

Complete the paragraph with prepositions.

Fuyi has a fish tank full _____ colorful tropical fish. These fish swim _____ rocks and hide _____ small caves. Fuyi feeds them special fish food that she got _____ a pet store.

Write a concluding statement for the narrative.

Mrs. DeMille was hosting a wedding in her backyard for her best friends, Josh and Sara. The weather was perfect. The cake was beautiful. The guests were all enjoying themselves. There was only one problem. Mrs. DeMille's dog, Daisy, had run away that morning. Mrs. DeMille was very worried. Then, the wedding march began. The bride walked down the aisle. She and the groom exchanged their vows. Just then, Daisy showed up and began trotting down the aisle.

_____

_____

_____

Spell the words correctly.

admitt _____

alagator _____

ansesstor _____

ancor _____

astronot _____

Many Icelandic settlers built **their** longhouses out of turf.

**adverb**      **possessive pronoun**

My big brother, _____ loves playing baseball, is teaching me the rules of the game.

Circle the relative pronouns. Underline the relative adverbs.

Concord, where the American Revolution began when the British and the colonists clashed, is a very pretty town in Massachusetts. It was also the home of Louisa May Alcott, who wrote *Little Women*, which is still read today and has been made into many movies.

Write a conclusion to the story.

Winslow was a horse that did not like to be kept in a barn. He wanted to be outside where he could gallop or graze on sweet clover. He looked at the water faucet above his water bucket. Slowly, he used his teeth to turn the knob of the faucet.

_____
_____
_____

Place a ✓ by each synonym.

**give**

❐ pass
❐ leave
❐ donate
❐ hand over
❐ sell
❐ lend

You (can, may, must) not forget to put the milk back in the refrigerator.

jenna loved to listen to the songs from an old musical called *my fair lady*.

Place a ✓ by each antonym.

**give**

❐ get
❐ take
❐ hold onto
❐ show
❐ receive
❐ keep

Think of one of your favorite animals. If that animal were a person, what kind of job would he be good at? How hard would he work at the job?

_____
_____
_____
_____
_____

_____ breakfast is ready.

**Your**

**You're**

Olivia asked (me, myself) what I thought of her story.

She wasn't sure if she liked it (her, herself).

---

That washing old machine still works very well.

That old washing machine still works very well.

---

Do you think students learn more from books or more from movies? Give reasons to support your opinion.

_____
_____
_____
_____
_____
_____
_____
_____
_____

---

Find and circle four words for **talk quietly**.

| W | Q | U | A | T | E | W |
|---|---|---|---|---|---|---|
| X | M | S | R | O | N | H |
| M | U | T | T | E | R | I |
| K | R | J | O | K | A | S |
| I | M | A | E | I | O | P |
| M | U | M | B | L | E | E |
| T | R | A | K | U | R | R |
| T | R | O | Y | A | U | E |

---

Maia was so _____ that she felt like **an old shoe**.

◯ **worn out**

◯ **full of holes**

◯ **comfortable**

---

**Time** and **thyme** are homophones. What vowel sound does **thyme** have?

---

◯ **usuall**

◯ **usual**

◯ **useal**

---

My best friend, _____ I visited yesterday, now lives in a different city.

---

You cannot see what is _____.

**misvisible**     **invisible**     **disvisible**

List three words you would use in a report about skateboarding.

_____

_____

_____

Rewrite the sentence correctly.

i won't start the engine until everyone is in the car

_____

_____

My grandfather's eyes _____ like stars when he opened his gift.

**shined     twinkled**

Years ago, when people had illnesses that spread quickly, they would be placed in **quarantine** in the hospital or at home. Circle the meaning of **quarantine**.

**a place where people spread illnesses**

**a place where people must stay to prevent the spread of illness**

   Ralph ran down the hall to the school auditorium. He lost track of the time and forgot that the tryouts for the school play were that evening. When he stumbled into the auditorium, the names of the people being selected for parts were being read. Ralph sighed, "I guess I **missed the boat** on that one."

What does the idiom mean?

_____

_____

_____

Spell the word correctly.

**biurst**

_____

   A volunteer helps people who need assistance or are in trouble. Volunteers do not get paid for their service. Have you ever volunteered for anything? If not, what kind of volunteer work might you enjoy someday? Write an informational piece about a real or imagined experience as a volunteer.

_____

_____

_____

_____

_____

_____

_____

_____

**berch**

**burch**

**birch**

examples
of
suffixes

Apples, berries, corn at the farmers market

**fragment**          **run-on**

Number the order of events in this story.

____ He scored a point!

____ It was his first time playing basketball for the team.

____ He threw the basketball to the hoop.

____ Neal was very nervous.

Circle the three words that best describe different ways an animal can move quickly.

**stagger**

**scamper**

**trudge**

**gallop**

**bolt**

Complete the synonym.

**plan to**

i__t__ __ __ __

Circle the most descriptive words.

Jared was (making, cooking) dinner. First, he (chopped, cut up) the vegetables before he (put, roasted) them in the oven. He then (tore, shredded) some lettuce leaves for a salad. Finally, he (made, baked) a cake.

Write a paragraph about a special hobby you enjoy. When did you first discover you liked it? Do you participate in or share your hobby with others? Why or why not?

_____

_____

_____

_____

_____

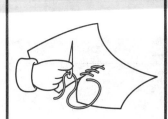

◯ **sew**

◯ **sow**

You will find *Matilda* in the _____ section.

**childrens**          **children's**          **childrens'**

My great aunt, _____ I admire very much, was once an airline pilot.

---

Circle the words that would most likely be used in an Internet search about astronauts.

Astronauts prepare to go into space by working in a simulator, which is a special chamber designed to operate just like a spaceship traveling in outer space.

---

Finally, place a pretty vase of flowers or an attractive centerpiece on top of the tablecloth.

Where would this sentence belong in an informational piece on how to set a dinner table?

○ **in the introduction**

○ **in a heading**

○ **in the conclusion**

---

Place a ✓ by each synonym.

**bright**

☐ smart

☐ glow

☐ dazzling

☐ shiny

☐ hot

☐ future

---

The copper shiny kettle is on the stove.

The shiny copper kettle is on the stove.

---

I (will, would) be able to read music by the end of my lessons.

---

Place a ✓ by each antonym.

**bright**

☐ rocky

☐ amuse

☐ shady

☐ lit

☐ dark

☐ dull

---

Write a conclusion to the story.

Tarike needed help learning how to play soccer so that she could try out for the team. She was new to the school and too shy to ask someone to teach her. Suddenly, she had an idea!

_____

_____

_____

_____

---

_____ going to the library to return those books, correct?

**Your**

**You're**

Evan looked for the memory card (that, which) held all of the photos from (his, its) beach trip. (He, It) was nowhere to be found.

---

I _____ walking home with my best friend who said he _____ _____ playing soccer tomorrow.

---

Circle **L** for literal or **F** for figurative.

**catch** the bus at Bowl Street          L          F

**sort** the students by name          L          F

**throw** the ball across the room          L          F

**ring** the bell at noon          L          F

**dig** for information          L          F

**sing** her brother's praises          L          F

**pull out** a tooth          L          F

---

Find and circle four words for **talk loudly**.

| Z | S | A | P | U | B | R |
|---|---|---|---|---|---|---|
| S | C | R | E | A | M | E |
| I | R | T | O | E | R | T |
| B | E | L | L | O | V | Y |
| A | E | U | Q | T | | R |
| K | C | R | Y | E | | E |
| J | H | O | L | N | T | S |

---

Circle the relative adverb.

Mrs. Tremonte, whose hous... around the corner, would like ... know when and where you are having your next school fund-raiser.

---

**fallback**

◯ a future plan

◯ a second best idea

---

Spell the word correctly.

**scaile**

_____

---

Barbara, _____ tea party was today, had a lovely time.

---

clarify = to make clear

purify = to make pure

simplify = _____

Circle the two synonyms. Use one in a sentence.

**restart**   **check**   **test**   **exact**

_____

_____

Rewrite the sentence correctly.

ray has a new mower which he keeps in the shed

_____

_____

They are putting a _____ _____ court in my neighborhood park.

**basketball**        **new**

Mrs. Ito's class had an **exhibition** in which all of their arts and crafts were displayed to the whole school.

Circle the meaning of **exhibition**.

**a public showing of items, usually artwork**

**a school that shows off artwork**

Christy's dad finished dinner early. "I'm sorry I can't shoot hoops with you tonight," his dad said. "But, we will do it tomorrow. Tonight, I have to finish a report for my work, and it looks like I will be **burning the midnight oil**."

What does the idiom mean?

_____

_____

_____

_____

○ **visible**

○ **vizable**

○ **visable**

You are writing a report on the history of women in America receiving the right to vote in 1920. Which facts and images should you use in your report?

○ **A.** an image of a ballot box from a current voting station

○ **B.** a photograph of women marching in support of the vote

○ **C.** a quote by a US senator stating why he was against the vote

○ **D.** a picture of a woman standing in front of the White House

○ **E.** a quote from a women's club against women voting

**horrify**

○ make someone less scared

○ make someone scared

Circle the correct prefix to complete the underlined word part in each sentence.

Sara thought the silly poem by Lewis Carroll was complete (non, un)<u>sense</u>.

While looking at the sky, Rosario saw a blue jay fly (under, over)<u>head</u>.

Chen's older brother rode his (bi, oct)<u>cycle</u> to school every day last week.

First drafts of stories and essays are normally (perfect, imperfect).

The idiom **"We'll cross that bridge when we come to it"** means

_____

_____

_____.

Millicent **laughed** at the funny song.

Write three other descriptive words or phrases for **laughed**.

_____

_____

_____

Complete the synonym.

**fortunate**

___ uc___ ___

Fill in the blanks with appropriate prepositions.

Tonya's dog Dizzy ran _____ the yard. Then, he jumped _____ a small fence before he plopped _____ the ground.

Write a concluding sentence for the narrative.

After spending months learning how to dance, Aisha entered a local talent show. Aisha was very nervous as she stepped onstage. Many other excellent people had danced before her, but she was determined to do her best. The music began.

_____

_____

_____

Spell the words correctly.

crum

_____

freckel

_____

exploar

_____

Page's _____ gave her a card for her birthday.

**Uncle        uncle**

Cristos, _____ picture was in the school newsletter last week, won an award for his artwork.

anchor captain cod eighteenth century nets New England ocean

Which topic would use all of the words in the word bank?

◯ how to learn to sail in 10 easy lessons

◯ the history of fishing in the United States

◯ protecting wildlife in the ocean today

---

Circle the transition words.

Making salad dressing is easy, plus it is less expensive than buying it in a store. First, gather your ingredients: mustard, vinegar, and olive oil. Then, put a small amount of mustard and vinegar in a bowl. Next, whip the two together into a fine mixture. Finally, slowly drizzle the oil into the mixture while you continue to whip the ingredients together. Voilà! You have salad dressing!

---

Place a ✓ by each synonym.

**grew**

☐ seeded

☐ tulip

☐ sprouted

☐ pled

☐ sprung up

☐ rooted

---

I _____ _____ hosting the talent show next weekend.

I _____ hosting the talent show this afternoon.

I _____ hosting the talent show last Saturday.

---

Bianca wrote a thank-you letter to her grandmother, _____ had sent her three books by her favorite author.

---

Place a ✓ by each word with the vowel sound in **toe**.

☐ **posted**

☐ **tossing**

☐ **loosely**

☐ **choices**

☐ **toasting**

☐ **stomach**

---

Harriet's class was asked to split into pairs to work on a science project on Friday. Harriet paired up with Chris because he was very smart. When Friday came, Chris was out with a cold. Harriet had to do all of the work herself!

Which proverb or adage sums up this situation?

◯ **A friend in need is a friend indeed.**

◯ **Too many cooks spoil the broth.**

◯ **Don't put all of your eggs in one basket.**

---

_____ the potatoes before you buy them at the market.

**Way**

**Weigh**

---

This chair is too tall for my desk, and I cannot fix it. I wish we had bought an (adjustable, adjuster) chair.

today mr humphries said a marine biologist will talk about whales in the pacific ocean

_____

_____

Write a conclusion the opinion piece.

   Over 100 years ago, President Theodore Roosevelt was responsible for passing legislation that protects much of our national park land today. Later, laws were passed by the government to protect a wide range wildlife. National parks are open to everyone, and for decades, people from all over the world have enjoyed their natural and amazing beauty. National parks have been used by the public for camping, hiking, and sightseeing. However, some business people see parks as wasted land that could be better used for houses and office buildings. They try to convince politicians to change the laws so that the land can become private property.

_____

_____

_____

Mark _____ studying all day yesterday, but he

_____ _____ playing softball with his friends later this afternoon.

Jennifer, who was

_____,

refused to come with us.

○ **as stubborn as a mule**

○ **as happy as a clam**

○ **as hungry as a horse**

aboard a _____

beyond the _____

underneath the _____

Spell the word correctly.

**thummb**

_____

Turn south to reach north dakota from here.

apologize = to make an apology

equalize = to make equal

tenderize = _____

List three words that you would use in a report about desert life.

_____

_____

_____

---

Rewrite the sentence correctly.

does anyone here have the time? asked cole

_____

_____

---

my older sister, leshawna, _____ loves history and english, _____ _____ starting at middlebury high school next year.

---

Her smiled sparkled like

_____.

---

Misty was very happy that it was the weekend. Every Saturday morning, her mother and she would find something fun to do in the area. When Misty asked her mom what she would like to do, her mom replied, "It's up to you. **The ball is in your court**."

What does the idiom mean?

_____

_____

_____

---

○ **mermaid**

○ **murmaid**

○ **mermade**

---

○ **diamonds**

○ **glass**

○ **water**

---

When we **memorize** something, we learn it by heart. We make sure we will not forget it.

Do you remember what -ize means? This might help: When we pluralize a word, we make the word plural. In just the same way, when we memorize a fact, we _____ the fact into a _____.

Write a different word with the -ize suffix and give its definition.

_____

_____

---

**chimpanzie**

**chimpanzey**

**chimpanzee**

---

Name _____  **Week 25, Day 1**

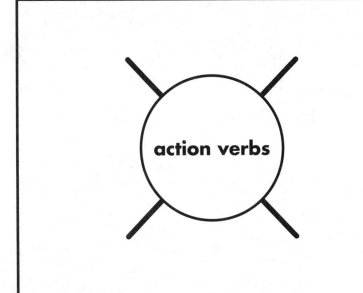

Antonyms (have similar, have opposite) meanings.

**alt-**
- ○ **land**
- ○ **life**
- ○ **high**

Place a ✓ by each linking word and phrases.
- ☐ **In addition**
- ☐ **For example**
- ☐ **To leave**
- ☐ **However**
- ☐ **Running**
- ☐ **Hardly**
- ☐ **Also**

- ○ **twelth**
- ○ **twelfth**
- ○ **twelvth**

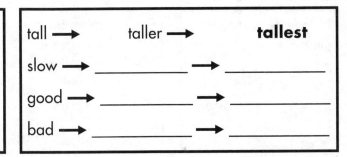

Circle the prepositions.

After breakfast, we got on the school bus. As usual, we went up the hill on Rose Street. Then, something strange happened. As we drove through the center of town, we saw a castle. Yes, a castle! It was standing in the middle of the town square. Nobody knew how it got there. Our driver shrugged. Then, she drove around the castle and took us to school.

- ○ **lead**
- ○ **led**

All three siblings got into the **blue old** car.

**correct order**    **incorrect order**

Add the missing punctuation.

"Stop___" she screamed.

Complete the sentence with the correct relative pronoun.

My ballet lessons, _____ are a lot of

fun, take place on Tuesdays.

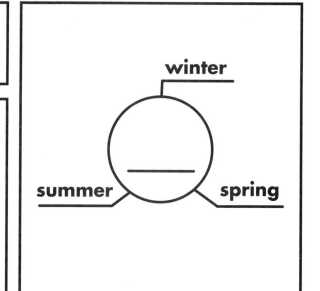

Place a ✓ by each synonym.

**gentle**

☐ laugh

☐ kind

☐ soft

☐ cheerful

☐ rapid

☐ manner

Circle the idiom.

It was raining cats and dogs.

The air is dusty and dirty.

He is as tall as a tree.

"Oh! A spider!" Grandma _____.

**shrieked   announced   replied**

Place a ✓ by each antonym.

**gentle**

☐ rough

☐ complain

☐ fearful

☐ worry

☐ ride

☐ harsh

Blake, Anthony, Maria, and Claire made pencil holders to sell at the school craft sale. They sold 46 pencil holders in all.

What information does the graph add to text?

_____

_____

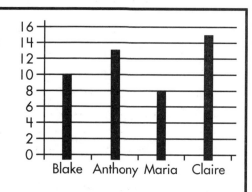

Write the suffix that can be added to each word.

peace____ ____ ____

care____ ____ ____

harm____ ____ ____

The lunch (which, that) he packed was too light.

He had a big snack (when, where) he got home.

---

Underline the word that has a prefix.

Kurt and Alexander both dislike dogs, so they stay away from them.

---

Circle **S** for simile or **M** for metaphor.

| | | |
|---|---|---|
| The river water looked like nasty cocoa. | S | M |
| The puppets were putty in the puppeteer's hands. | S | M |
| The moon was a half-eaten piece of cream pie. | S | M |
| The figure skater twirled around like a maple seed. | S | M |
| The first baseman had an arm of steel. | S | M |
| The hamster scurried like an ant. | S | M |

---

Say the name of the picture. Write a polysyllabic word that has the same vowel sound.

_____

---

Write three prepositions that begin with the letter *a*.

_____

_____

_____

---

Circle the cause. Underline the effect.

Animals seek shelter when they hear a storm coming.

---

Complete the synonym.

**lump**

b___ ___ge

---

Correct the title.

The Astronot goes to the Moon

---

My uncle owns a **big brown** dog.

**correct order**          **incorrect order**

New York City is an interesting place. You can see many things there, such as the Empire State Building. You can also visit Central Park. Many people like to drive over the Brooklyn Bridge.

This paragraph mainly (tells a story, teaches about a place).

---

Insert the missing comma.

I enjoy playing field hockey but I don't have time anymore.

---

Underline the word(s) with a **long a** sound.

We had a great time at the state carnival yesterday.

---

We do a lot of fun things in Mrs. Ortiz's class.

_____, we put on a play last month.

**In addition**

**For example**

---

My little sister Monique skipped into the room. She was humming to herself. She had a huge smile on her tiny face. It didn't matter that it was raining and we were stuck inside. Monique was still **cheerful**.

What is the meaning of **cheerful**? How do you know?

___  _____

___  _____

_  _____

_____

---

Spell the word corrrectly.

**singnal**

_____

---

A sunburn can be painful. Your skin can turn red, swell, itch, and peel. Nobody likes a sunburn! You can take steps to prevent getting sunburned. Using sunscreen is a great way to protect your skin. Also, you can wear a hat with a brim. You can even try staying indoors from 10:00 am and 4:00 pm on hot days. This is when the sun is the strongest.

○ **chronology**

○ **comparison**

○ **cause/effect**

○ **problem/solution**

---

English is an example of this two-syllable word.

I_____

synonyms for "yell"

A prefix is placed at the (beginning, end) of a word.

Place a dot (•) between syllables.

g r a t e f u l

f a n c i f u l

p o w e r f u l

Place a ✓ by each word with the same vowel sound.

☐ shriek

☐ spear

☐ soak

☐ sneeze

☐ sneak

☐ speck

Complete the synonym.

**damp**

m___ is___

Circle the stronger sentence.

Trevor went down the stairs.

Trevor flew down the stairs.

Circle the contractions. Then, write them as two separate words.

You won't believe what my sister and I saw today! We saw a spaceship right on our lawn. I'm not making this up! It had flashing lights and made a beeping noise. My sister said, "Let's check it out," so we knocked on the door. Nobody came out, so we're going to try again tonight.

_____          _____

_____          _____

_____          _____

_____          _____

○ main

○ mane

I have always said that strawberries are like rubies.

**simile          metaphor**

Correct the sentence.

"Are you going to the play" she asked.

---

Complete the paragraph using relative pronouns.

Last night, we ran into Jorge, _____ we hadn't seen in months! He was wearing the sweatshirt _____ I gave him. Jorge joined us on our trip to the park. He was with his older sister, _____ was happy to leave him with us, I think. It was all just like last summer, except for the snow, of course. We all made snowballs, _____ fell apart as soon as we threw them.

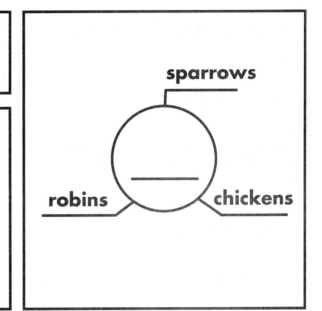

---

Place a ✓ by each synonym.

**command**

☐ stand

☐ order

☐ listen

☐ keep

☐ rule

☐ shout

---

Circle the idiom.

I had a change of heart.

Her skin was as cold as ice.

My legs are sore from running.

---

"I'm not going to the party, and that's final!"

Sonja _____.

**spoke    declared    revealed**

---

Place a ✓ by each antonym.

**command**

☐ speak

☐ answer

☐ ask

☐ find

☐ lose

☐ help

---

Amir, Billy, Jayne, and Marcella each read books for the library's reading contest. Jayne was the runaway winner.

Does the graph support the text? Why or why not?

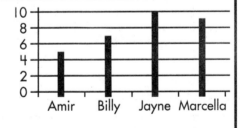

_____

_____

---

Write the suffix that can be added to each word.

quick____ ____

light____ ____

beautiful____ ____

Chloe broke her (heal, heel) bone when she fell.

The bone will take some time to (heal, heel).

---

Underline the word that has a prefix.

Anil thought that it was impossible to win the game, but he was wrong.

---

Circle **S** for sentence or **F** for fragment.

Josie ran to third base.                    S        F

I go to Ashland Elementary School.          S        F

Went to Crag Lake with my brother.          S        F

Your cousins are very nice.                 S        F

Plays soccer every weekend.                 S        F

The best flavor of pie.                     S        F

Did not finish my homework.                 S        F

---

Say the name of the picture. Write a three-syllable word that has the same vowel sound.

_____

---

Write three prepositions that begin with the letter *b*.

_____

_____

_____

---

Circle the cause. Underline the effect.

People who eat properly often stay healthy.

---

Spell the word correctly.

**obeay**

_____

---

Correct the title.

Mrs Gordon´s Garden

---

tele = far away

phone = sound

telephone = _____

Alan ran up the hill with his sled. He threw himself on top of the sled and flew down the hill. Suddenly, a snowball struck him on the back. Of course, it was his big brother, Devin!

This paragraph mainly (tells a story,

teaches about a place).

---

Circle the homophones.

Have you read this red book? You

should read it soon.

---

Underline the word(s) with a **long e** sound.

My family had a picnic down by the stream.

---

Lali used to live in Utah.

_____, she

used to live in Iowa.

**In addition**

**However**

---

My neighbor, Mr. Behr, stepped into his yard. "I can't believe it! Now what am I going to do? This is terrible!" he **bellowed**. I didn't blame him for being upset. The storm had tossed a huge tree branch across his car.

What is the meaning of **bellowed**? How do you know?

_____
_____
_____
_____

---

○ **glaring**

○ **glarring**

○ **glareing**

---

It is the year 1926, and you are staying at a hotel in the south of England. A hotel worker hands you a small tray with a piece of paper that says:

I bet you've never gotten one of these stop

I sent a telegram from Manchester stop

*"Stop" means "end of sentence."*

The suffix **-gram** means **writing**. What does **telegram** mean?

_____
_____

---

This two-syllable word means the opposite of **deep**.

s_____

antonyms
for
"enormous"

"The car was as clean as a whistle" is an example of a (metaphor, simile).

Place a dot (•) between syllables.

f r o z e n

f i g u r e

f l u t t e r e d

Place a ✓ by each word with the same vowel sound.

☐ **laugh**

☐ **tough**

☐ **rode**

☐ **shove**

☐ **bud**

☐ **pour**

Spell the word correctly.

**rangje**

_____

Circle the stronger sentence.

Javier put his finger in the pie.

Javier poked his finger in the pie.

Circle the misspelled words. Then, write them correctly.

   Last weekend, our town celabrated Founder's Day. Everyone ha
a great time—until the rain started poring down!  Naturaly, nobo
had an umbrela because the weather report said it was supposed t
be sunny. Everyone retreeted to their cars. What a newsance! May
next year will be better.

_____     _____

_____     _____

_____     _____

◯ **muscle**

◯ **mussel**

This two-syllable word can be a synonym for **new**, **fresh**, or **latest**.

m_____

Correct the sentence.
"We´re going to be late emma said.

_____

Complete the paragraph using relative pronouns.

   Nobody knows _____ project will win at the science fair. I would choose the water bottle terrariums, _____ were made by a third grader named Gwen. The judges usually give first prize to a student _____ has designed a nice poster board. It doesn´t look like Gwen put much effort into her display. The nicest poster belongs to Jayden, _____ I met at the fair this morning.

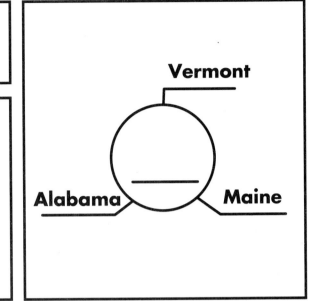

Place a ✓ by each synonym.

**quiet**

◻ low

◻ normal

◻ hushed

◻ silent

◻ soft

◻ whisper

Circle the idiom.

Aliya can run as fast as a tiger.

Jane has a shot at the blue ribbon.

Tomas will probably win the bike race.

"I got the lead in the school play!" Martin

_____.

**replied     stated     exclaimed**

Place a ✓ by each antonym.

**quiet**

◻ noisy

◻ hard

◻ faint

◻ heard

◻ loud

◻ easy

   Hector, Randy, Amelia, and LaTasha earned money doing chores for their neighbors. Hector and LaTasha earned more money than the other two. What information does the graph add to the text?

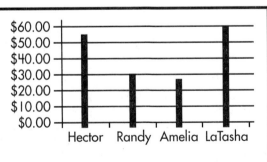

_____

_____

Write the suffix that can be added to each word.


kind___ ___ ___ ___


sweet___ ___ ___ ___


good___ ___ ___ ___

Riko felt as if she was (onto, in) a dream.

With her head up, she walked (onto, in) the field.

---

Underline the word that has a prefix.

I thought the class trip was today, but I was incorrect.

---

Circle **C** for correct or **I** for incorrect.

| | | |
|---|---|---|
| We will be arriving this afternoon. | C | I |
| The train is running on time. | C | I |
| Our trip will have been a lot of fun. | C | I |
| Our cousins are wait for us at the station. | C | I |
| We are excited we are going to the beach. | C | I |
| There are going to being a lot of people. | C | I |
| We will not be wanting to go home very soon. | C | I |

---

Say the name of the picture. Write a polysyllabic word that has the same vowel sound.

_____

---

Write three prepositions that begin with the letter *o*.

_____

_____

_____

---

Earth, Mars, and Saturn are examples of this two-syllable word.

p_____

---

Complete the antonym.

**shiny**

___ul___

---

Correct the title.

Tom´s Terible Tomatos

---

We saw **little yellow** chicks on the farm.

**correct order**          **incorrect order**

Bonnie was nervous to try out for the soccer team. She loved soccer, but she had never been on a team before. Even so, her mom had encouraged her to try. Now, Bonnie was standing on the edge of the field, waiting her turn.

This paragraph mainly (tells a story, teaches about a sport).

---

Circle the homographs.

Can you bear looking at a bear that

bares its teeth?

---

Underline the word(s) with a **long i** sound.

Antonio tried to lift the box, but it was too heavy.

---

It rained this afternoon.

_____, we

couldn't play in the yard.

**Therefore**

**For instance**

---

Tanya stood, staring at her feet. Bits of wood, paper, and cardboard were everywhere. She would have to explain to Mrs. Washington what had happened. She had tripped on the sidewalk, and now her project was **destroyed**.

What is the meaning of **destroyed**? How do you know?

_____

_____

_____

_____

---

○ **service**

○ **survice**

○ **servise**

---

Clouds are made up of tiny drops of water and bits of ice. The water and ice are so small and light that they can hang in the air. However, these drops grow bigger and bigger. They become the clouds we see up above. At some point, the drops get so big that they fall to Earth. Depending on the temperature, we can get rain or snow.

○ **chronology**

○ **comparison**

○ **cause/effect**

○ **problem/solution**

---

Someone who takes **photographs** is a

_____.

synonyms
for
"cheerful"

Stories and essays have paragraphs,

while poems have (lines, stanzas).

An **astronaut** is a person who

_____.

An **astronomer** is a person who

_____.

Place a ✓ by each
three-syllable word.

❏ **sentence**

❏ **protection**

❏ **magnet**

❏ **national**

❏ **responsible**

❏ **information**

Spell the word
correctly.

**colonny**

_____

Circle the stronger sentence.

Jasmine ran through the park.

Jasmine raced through the park.

Circle the homophones. Then, write the homophone pair for each
word circled.

   Yesterday, I went to the beach with my uncle. I took my pail so that
I could build a sand castle. There were a lot of sand castles on the
beach, but mine was the biggest! "Can we come back here?" I asked
my uncle as we were leaving.

_____     _____

_____     _____

_____     _____

_____     _____

◯ **doe**

◯ **dough**

The root *fract-* means **break**. What word means part of a number?

_____

Correct the sentence.
"Do you want to come to my house" todd asked.

_____

Complete the sentences with the correct relative pronouns.

I spoke with Tom, _____ I know from camp.

I admired his bike, _____ was exactly like the one I want.

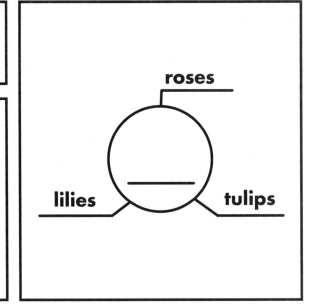

roses

lilies          tulips

Place a ✓ by each synonym.

**suspect**

❏ feel

❏ know

❏ think

❏ tell

❏ guess

❏ sense

Circle the adage.

Reading books can make you smarter.

A good book is like a good friend.

Don´t judge a book by its cover.

As the puppy raced out the front door,

Caroline _____ after him.

**stepped      wandered      tore**

Place a ✓ by the prepositions.

❏ **with**

❏ **outside**

❏ **behind**

❏ **were**

❏ **across**

❏ **during**

❏ **few**

Miss Tan´s class took a poll to find out the students´ favorite sports. Most of her students preferred winter sports to summer sports.

Does the graph support the text? Why or why not?

_____

_____

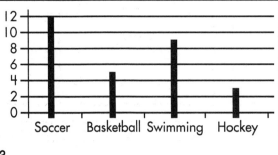

Write the suffix that can be added to each word.

box___ ___

peach___ ___

bush___ ___

Many types of pine trees grow (in, along) North America.

Red pines grow (in, along) the coast of New England.

---

Underline the word that has a prefix.

If Mrs. Kapoor's class misbehaves, they are not allowed to have recess.

---

Circle **S** for sentence or **F** for fragment.

Share a room with my sister.            **S**      **F**

Craig is much taller than I am.         **S**      **F**

Wanted to go to the play, but I didn't.   **S**      **F**

Sheryl is in my class this year.        **S**      **F**

Raises tomatoes in her backyard.        **S**      **F**

We met the new neighbors, who are very nice.   **S**      **F**

Did not attend the concert.             **S**      **F**

---

Say the name of the picture. Write a three-syllable word that has the same vowel sound.

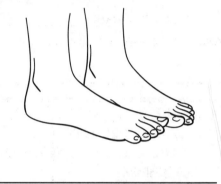

_____

Write three prepositions that begin with the letter *t*.

_____

_____

_____

---

Circle the cause. Underline the effect.

People can catch colds if they do not bundle up in cold weather.

---

○ **relief**

○ **releif**

○ **releaf**

---

Correct the title.

pluto, the dwarf planet

---

They left the rolled-up plans **on the far table**.

**correct**          **incorrect**

When I visited my uncle in Wyoming, I saw a beaver. It was small and brown. It had huge teeth and a flat tail. My uncle said a beaver's home is called a lodge. Beavers build lodges on the water. Beavers are interesting to watch.

This paragraph mainly (tells a story about a trip teaches about an animal).

They said (its, it's) hard (to, too, two) understand the movie.

_____

_____

Underline the word(s) with a **long o** sound.

We rowed the boat to the other shore.

I don't like basketball.

_____, I

quit the team.

**As a result**

**However**

The root *bio-* means "life." In science, **biology** is the study of all life. A **biologist** is someone who studies biology.

A **biography** is _____

_____.

A **biographer** is someone who

_____

_____

_____

_____.

Complete the antonym.

**rough**

s___ ___ ___th

When places don't get enough rain, a drought can occur. Droughts make it hard for farmers to water their crops. The worst droughts can make it hard for people to get water to drink.

People can do things to save water. They can turn off the tap when they're brushing their teeth. They can fill bathtubs only halfway. They can stop washing their cars. These steps can be helpful if a drought occurs.

○ **chronology**

○ **comparison**

○ **cause/effect**

○ **problem/solution**

This two-syllable word can be a synonym for **create**, **make**, or **design**.

i_____

Complete the acrostic poem.

**Moose**

A _____

M _____

M _____

A _____

L _____

In a drama, actors are given lines to speak. This is called the (dialogue, stage direction).

Place a dot (•) between syllables.

t h r o u g h o u t

d u r i n g

a f t e r w a r d

Place a ✓ by each synonym.

**large**

❏ huge

❏ thin

❏ enormous

❏ short

❏ giant

❏ shallow

◯ **nonsence**

◯ **noncents**

◯ **nonsense**

Circle the stronger sentence.

Hoshi gazed at the stars.

Hoshi looked at the stars.

Circle each word that should begin with a capital letter. Then, write the word correctly above it.

   Last saturday, uncle toby visited from texas. He took me to the zoo.

We saw a big cat called a cheetah. Her name was spotty. After the

zoo, we went out for ice cream. "Did you have a good time?" mom

asked when we got home. "Yes!" i told her.

◯ **moose**

◯ **mousse**

In poetry, the last word of each line rhymes with another.

**true          false          sometimes true**

Correct the sentence.

Are you bringing brownies sarah asked.

---

Complete the sentences with the correct relative pronouns.

Everyone _____ is going on the trip

should board the bus now.

The bus we will board is the big green one

_____ is parked in front.

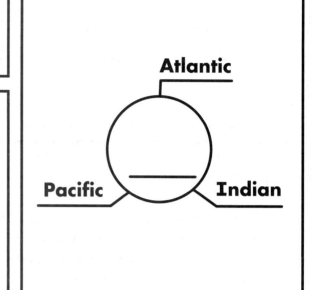

---

Place a ✓ by each synonym.

**rush**

❏ dash

❏ hurry

❏ race

❏ walk

❏ bolt

❏ traffic

---

Circle the adage.

I admitted that I was wrong.

Two wrongs don't make a right.

He got one wrong answer on the test.

---

Ana's softball bat _____ against the ball as she hit a home run.

**cracked    hit    bumped**

---

Place a ✓ by each antonym.

**rush**

❏ near

❏ delay

❏ seat

❏ wait

❏ far

❏ last

---

Mr. Alcott's class took a poll to find out what kind of pets each student's family owned. Can you infer from this graph that more of Mr. Alcott's students own cats than dogs?

Why or why not?

_____

_____

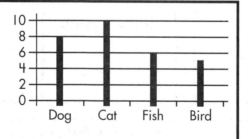

---

Find the suffix that can be added to all three words. Complete the words.

run__ __ __ __

drag__ __ __ __

sit__ __ __ __

---

Ethan finished earlier (than, then) I did.

He (than, then) waited for me to catch

up before moving on.

---

Underline the word that has a prefix.

My aunt is making preparations for her wedding,

which is in April.

---

Dear Charlie,

   I'm sorry I was not able to go to the shore this weekend. All day on Saturday, I was thinking of you and Phuong and how you must have been basking in the sun. I hope I can come the next time you make the trip!

                              Your friend,
                              Maddie

P.S. Those pictures you sent me looked great!

"P.S." stands for **postscript**. If *post-* means "after," then **postscript** means

_____ .

---

Say the name of the picture. Write a three-syllable word that has the same vowel sound.

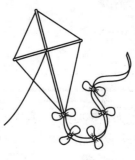

_____

---

Write three prepositions that begin with the letter *u*.

_____

_____

_____

---

Circle the cause. Underline the effect.

When winter comes, it snows.

---

Complete the synonym.

**hold tightly**

___ ri ___

---

Correct the title.

How To Suceed In Writing

---

The **white fat** cat jumped on the chair.

**correct order**          **incorrect order**

My sister has a garden. She grows tulips. Tulips bloom in the spring. They come in many colors such as red, yellow, and orange. My sister waters her tulips every day and gives them plant food so that they will stay healthy.

This paragraph mainly (teaches about tulips, tells a story about a girl who loves tulips).

---

Insert the missing commas.

I do not like basketball nor do I like football.

I like baseball but no one else in my family does.

---

Underline the word(s) with a **long u** sound.

Do your homework before you go out to play.

---

In a play, actors have to speak their lines, which are written

○ **on a clipboard.**

○ **in a script.**

○ **on the pages of a book.**

---

Jaden spotted Mr. Walker's groceries sitting on the curb. Using his cane, Mr. Walker was slowly climbing his front steps. He was taking one bag at a time. Jaden grabbed a bag and climbed the steps too. He felt good that he had done a good **deed**.

What is the meaning of **deed**? How do you know?

_____

_____

_____

---

Spell the word correctly.

**casstle**

_____

---

Both cats and dogs make good pets, but they're very different. Cats don't need to be walked like dogs do. For this reason, cats can be easier to take care of. However, cats probably won't play fetch with you like a dog will. Most house cats are small, but dogs can be many sizes. People need to decide if a cat or dog is better for them and their families.

○ **chronology**

○ **comparison**

○ **cause/effect**

○ **problem/solution**

---

This two-syllable word is a synonym for **fight** or **argue**.

q _____

Circle the words that relate to the **cold**.

| | | |
|---|---|---|
| wriggle | numb | pout |
| lakefront | grove | glacier |
| subzero | bitter | stuck |

Our normal, everyday speech is more like (prose, poetry) than (prose, poetry)

Place a dot (•) between syllables.

t e l e g r a p h

a u t o g r a p h

b i o g r a p h y

Place a ✓ by each word that should be capitalized.

- ☐ **september**
- ☐ **monday**
- ☐ **museum**
- ☐ **school**
- ☐ **doctor**
- ☐ **florida**

Complete the synonym.

**to utter**

___o___ce

Circle the stronger sentence.

Patrick looked at the pie on the counter.

Patrick eyed the pie on the counter.

Underline the sentence fragments. Then, rewrite them as complete sentences.

My best friend's name is Betsy. She and I like to my house after school. Sometimes, we watch movies. Other times we trees. Yesterday, we decided to write our own play and perform it. We always have a lot of fun together. I'm really glad that Betsy is my best friend.

_____

_____

_____

○ fourth

○ forth

(After, During, Through) the ceremony, we will be going out to a fancy restaurant.

Name _____    **Week 30, Day 2**

Correct the sentence.

"We won the game javier exclaimed

Complete the paragraph using relative adverbs.

  A sinking feeling came _____ I saw my brother´s report card. He had even aced geometry! I didn´t know _____ I expected him to do poorly or _____ I hoped so! I thought my parents would be less upset with me if we both had low grades. I cringed _____ I saw my report card in the mail. Mother smiled _____ she was through reading it. I´d done just fine!

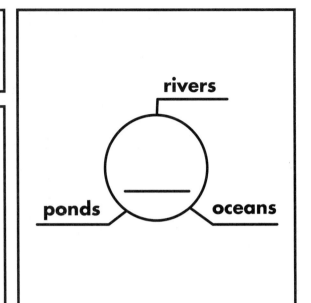

Place a ✓ by each synonym.

**old**

□ worn
□ poor
□ high
□ wise
□ lengthy
□ aged

Circle the adage.

That crow was as big as my cat.

There are birds that do not fly.

The early bird gets the worm.

My three-year-old sister Marisol

_____ around the room to the music.

**shifted    pranced    moved**

Place a ✓ by each antonym.

**old**

□ recent
□ born
□ soon
□ latest
□ modern
□ current

Replace the incorrect words with their antonyms.

The desert was bustling that afternoon. Many plants dotted the landscape. The sun shone so dully that I had to shield my eyes. Most of the animals of the desert were in hiding, waiting for the warm evening.

Write the suffix that can be added to each word.

hair___

curl___

storm___

134    © Carson-Dellosa • CD-104878

Do you know (who, whom) the movie is about?

It is about Ada Lincoln, (who, whom) was an early programmer.

---

Underline the word that has a prefix.

We had to remove our books from our desks at the end of the school year.

---

Circle **S** for sentence or **R** for run-on.

Let's to go Marley's house before dinner.                    S     R

I'm going to the store, if you'd like to come along.          S     R

Teddy caught the ball, but then he dropped it.                S     R

Malik went bike riding Sondra went with him.                  S     R

Don't go outside it's raining and you'll get wet.            S     R

I can't remember what chapter we need to read.               S     R

Patches is my cat I love her very much.                      S     R

---

Say the name of the picture. Write a three-syllable word that has the same vowel sound.

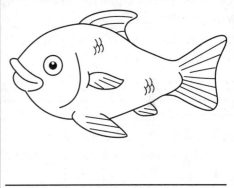

_____

---

Write three adjectives that describe what you see outside of the window right now.

_____

_____

_____

---

Circle the cause. Underline the effect.

People stay in shape when they

get a lot of exercise.

---

Spell the word correctly.

**snieak**

_____

---

Correct the title.

    The Bear and Her Cub's

---

My **red old** shirt is very comfortable.

**correct order**          **incorrect order**

---

We spent the summer in Florida with my grandma. We went on picnics and went swimming. I loved splashing around in the clear blue water. It was the best time I ever had.

This paragraph mainly (tells a story about a trip,

teaches about a place).

---

Rewrite the sentence correctly.

Yes Kyra agreed we'll camp out in the morning.

_____

_____

---

Underline the word(s) with a **short a** sound.

Patches, my orange cat, eats her food on the back porch.

---

Fara finished her book report after school.

_____, she did her math homework.

**While**

**Then**

---

Curtis had never been in his grandma's basement before. He poked his head around the stacks of boxes. Then, he looked in the space under the stairs. He even opened some old books. Curtis loved **exploring**.

What is the meaning of **exploring**? How do you know?

_____

_____

_____

_____

---

○ **solger**

○ **soldier**

○ **soldjer**

---

Beatrix Potter was a famous author. She was born in England more than 150 years ago. She wrote many works for children. In 1902, Beatrix published her first book, *The Tale of Peter Rabbit*. She later wrote another animal book called *The Tale of Squirrel Nutkin*, which came out in 1903. The next year, she wrote *The Tale of Benjamin Bunny*. Beatrix Potter wrote many books that children still love today.

○ **chronology**

○ **comparison**

○ **cause/effect**

○ **problem/solution**

---

This three-syllable word is the opposite of **forget**.

_____

Fill in the blanks with prepositions.

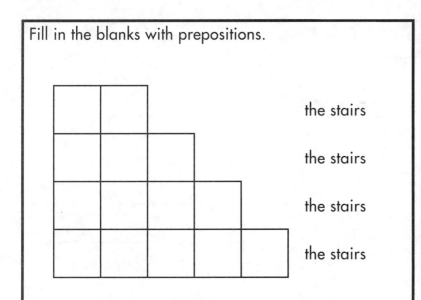

_____ the stairs

_____ the stairs

_____ the stairs

_____ the stairs

The narrator of a story determines the story's (point of view, setting).

Place a dot (•) between syllables.

p a r t i c u l a r

p r o n o u n c e

p r o t e c t i o n

Place a ✓ by each word that should be lowercased.

☐ **December**

☐ **Tuesday**

☐ **Mother**

☐ **Student**

☐ **Math**

☐ **Iowa**

Spell the word correctly.

**servicse**

_____

Circle the stronger sentence.

Lucinda dashed toward the school bus.

Lucinda ran toward the school bus.

Circle the run-on sentences. Then, rewrite them as complete sentences.

   I really like reading books they can take you to places you can't go in real life. For example, you can go to other planets you can go back in time or to other countries. Books allow you to pretend you are somebody else for a little while. Also, they let you learn things you never knew before. You can learn about new people, places, and things.

_____

_____

_____

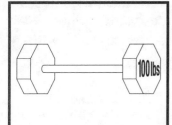

○ **weight**

○ **wait**

Mel took a karate class _____ autumn.

**along**　　**during**　　**past**

Correct the sentence.

My school, lee elementary school, is on main street

Complete the sentences with the correct relative pronouns.

Apples, _____ are delicious, can grow in New York.

The environment, _____ includes the soil and climate, is perfect.

science

math

language arts

Place a ✓ by each synonym.

**near**

❑ handy

❑ close by

❑ on top of

❑ neighbor

❑ come

❑ there

Circle the adage.

He was ahead of me in the lunch line.

I am going to head over to the park.

Two heads are better than one.

We _____ into the bedroom to hide the presents.

**sneaked     went     marched**

Place a ✓ by each antonym.

**near**

❑ there

❑ far

❑ distant

❑ a long way

❑ other

❑ different

Fiona came down with a bad illness last Friday. She felt miserable, with a sore throat, aching head, and goosebumps all over. The fact that she got sick right before the weekend only **amplified** how poorly she felt. She was supposed to go on a trip that weekend with her friends. Instead, she would be stuck at home, wishing she was spending time with her friends.

What does **amplified** mean in this paragraph?

_____

_____

Write the suffix that can be added to each word.

govern__ __ __ __

state__ __ __ __

announce__ __ __ __

We (must, may) laugh more when we are all together.

Andrew (can, must) laugh loudest of all.

---

Underline the word that has a prefix.

Alyssa thought it was unfair that she wasn´t allowed to go to the movies with Mia.

---

Tony waved his hands frantically, trying to catch Mel's attention. She watched as Tony made sign after mysterious sign. He made a *D* with his hands—*Dad*. He held up an index finger—*won*. He stumbled over an invisible rock—*a trip*. He held up two fingers—*to*. At last, he tried his best to mime the throwing of tea crates into a harbor—*Boston*. It wasn´t the best game of charades ever played, but few have had to try in the middle of a softball game.

How might this story be different if it were told in the first person from Mel´s point of view?

_____

_____

_____

_____

---

Say the name of the picture. Write a polysyllable word that has the same vowel sound.

_____

---

Write three verbs in the past tense.

_____

_____

_____

---

Circle the cause. Underline the effect.

Children do not do well in school if they stay up too late.

---

Complete the antonym.

**mumble**

___ho___t

---

Correct the title.

The Three Branches of Goverment

---

I cut my hand on a **sharp big** rock.

**correct order**   **incorrect order**

There are many different kinds of birds. Some birds, such as flamingos, are large. Others, such as finches, are small. Different birds live in different parts of the world. It is very interesting to learn about birds.

This paragraph mainly (describes the author's feelings, gives details on a topic).

---

When the narrator of a story is also one of the characters, the story is written in (first, third) person.

When the narrator of a story is not one of the characters, the story is written in (first, third) person.

---

Underline the word(s) with a **short e** sound.

We put jelly on our bread, which we ate in the kitchen.

---

Izumi used to take flute lessons. _____, she plays the drums.

---

photo-          not

bi-             light

tri-            wrongly

quad-           two

mis-            too little

non-            three

under-          four

---

○ **Main St**

○ **Main ST.**

○ **Main St.**

---

**After**

**Now**

---

George Washington was born in 1732. He was born in Virginia. He mostly grew up on Ferry Farm, also in Virginia. At the age of 15, he left school. Washington later became a soldier. He fought in the American Revolution. He helped the army fight against the British soldiers. Later, George Washington went on to become the first president of the United States.

Is this paragraph informative or argumentative? How do you know?

_____

_____

_____

_____

_____

---

This three-syllable word is a synonym for **lucky**.

f_____

Circle the words that relate to **thinking**.

| consider | wonder | rustle |
|----------|--------|--------|
| change | utensil | immense |
| reflect | sneak | review |

Insert the missing comma.

Do you want to go swimming or would you rather go on a picnic?

Place a dot (•) between syllables.

s e t t i n g

c h a r a c t e r

e v e n t

Place a ✓ by each word that uses the punctuation correctly.

☐ **won't**

☐ **shouldn't**

☐ **wev'e**

☐ **its'**

☐ **Iv'e**

☐ **I'm**

○ **cabbiage**

○ **cabbage**

○ **cabbige**

Circle the stronger sentence.

Lilly dangled the yarn in front of the cat.

Lilly held the yarn in front of the cat.

Insert commas in the correct places.

    My family has a garden. We grow a lot of flowers. For example we grow roses daisies and tulips. In addition we grow tomatoes. Mom and I do most of the watering. On the weekend Dad and my sister do the weeding. Gardens can be a lot of fun but they are also a lot of hard work.

○ warn

○ worn

We kept the news a secret, but Lee **let the cat out of the bag**.

**simile**          **metaphor**

Name _____

**Name** _____  **Week 32, Day 2**

Correct the sentence.

My cousin helen is going to new york city on friday.

Complete the paragraph using relative pronouns.

We discussed our favorite fruits. Grapes are the fruit _____ I like least, but Mike likes them best. There was no one at our table _____ liked grapefruit. Many liked other citrus fruits. Bethany loves oranges, _____ she packs in her lunch every day. I asked to trade a few grapes for an orange slice, but she said, "There is nothing _____ I would exchange for my orange."

carrots / potatoes / peas _____

Place a ✓ by each synonym.

**plan**

☐ find out
☐ lay out
☐ sketch
☐ plot
☐ repeat
☐ design

Circle the adage.

There are many different kinds of dogs.

My cat looks just like the cat down the street.

Don't count your chickens before they're hatched.

Oscar _____ his feet on the ground, unwilling to move.

**planted**    **set**    **left**

Place a ✓ by each relative pronoun.

☐ **then**
☐ **whose**
☐ **that**
☐ **why**
☐ **which**
☐ **when**

Think of something you learned recently in another class. Introduce the topic for someone who knows very little about it.

_____
_____
_____
_____

Write the suffix that can be added to each word.

neighbor__ __ __ __

child__ __ __ __

state__ __ __ __

I knew every answer on the test (accept, except) the last one.

I had to (accept, except) the grade I earned.

---

Underline the word that has a prefix.

I told Mr. Bellman that my homework had disappeared, but he didn't believe me.

---

Circle **S** for simile or **M** for metaphor.

| | | |
|---|---|---|
| My sister is an animal on the hockey rink. | S | M |
| The beach ball was as big as a watermelon. | S | M |
| The snow is a blanket over the meadow. | S | M |
| When my friends come over, my house is a zoo. | S | M |
| She rides her bike as fast as a cheetah. | S | M |
| The classroom was a freezer in December. | S | M |
| After it rained, the parking lot was like a lake. | S | M |

---

Say the name of the picture. Write a polysyllable word that has the same vowel sound.

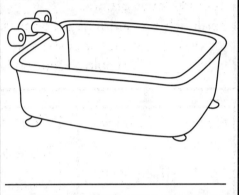

_____

This book is most likely

**informative**

**fiction**

---

Circle the cause. Underline the effect.
The sport rugby was invented in England, but then it started being played in other countries.

---

Spell the word correctly.

**shallouw**

_____

---

Correct the title.

Animals and There Young

---

The monster had **bulging big** eyes.

**correct order**     **incorrect order**

I don't like dogs. Dogs are scary. Many of them are big and have sharp teeth. It's also scary when they bark loudly. Also, I think it's disgusting when dogs lick your face! I'd never own a dog.

This paragraph mainly (gives details on a topic, describes the author's feelings).

I don't know (who's, whose) biography I should read for class.

Underline the word(s) with a **short i** sound.

I left my homework in my room, so I decided to run home at lunch and get it.

John likes climbing trees.

_____, he likes playing board games.

**Next**

**Also**

in-          life
over-        ten
tele-        not
graph-       hundred
bio-         under
centi-       far
deca-        too much
sub-         written

Complete the synonym.

**plunge**

___ iv ___

People often confuse crocodiles and alligators. However, they are different in many ways. For example, their snouts have different shapes. Crocodiles have longer, thinner snouts. Alligators have shorter, rounder snouts. When a crocodile closes its mouth, some of its teeth can still be seen. When an alligator closes its mouth, its teeth are hidden.

The last two sentences of this paragraph look very much alike. How does that help the author show how these two animals are different?

_____

_____

_____

_____

This three-syllable word means **to give up**.

s _____

Draw and write the names of six punctuation marks.

| | | |
|---|---|---|
| | | |
| | | |

You (can, cannot) understand an idiom just by looking at the words.

Place a dot (•) between syllables.

c o n t a i n

e n c o u r a g e

p u r p o s e

Place a ✓ by each preposition.

☐ **on**

☐ **over**

☐ **through**

☐ **then**

☐ **later**

☐ **quickly**

○ **pottary**

○ **pottery**

○ **pottury**

Circle the stronger sentence.

Jose's eyes bulged out of his head.

Jose's eyes opened wide.

Circle the words and phrases that describe the story's setting.

Juan ran ahead while Ricardo tossed down his soccer ball. Today was a great day to play in the park. The sun was shining through the puffy, white clouds. The grassy field was completely empty. The boys could play until dinner. Suddenly, a rumbling came from up above. "Oh, no," said Juan. "Oh, yes," said Ricardo, pointing to the gray clouds that had formed. The boys ran home.

○ **desert**

○ **dessert**

_____ baseball glove is on the bench?

**Who**      **Whom**      **Whose**

Correct the sentence.

My grandma is teaching me to speak italian.

---

Complete the sentences with the correct relative pronouns.

Music is the subject _____ I love the most.

I sing in a choir, _____ practices every Tuesday after school.

---

watermelon

strawberries          plums

---

Place a ✓ by each synonym.

**brave**

❑ careful

❑ plucky

❑ excited

❑ misfortune

❑ unafraid

❑ bold

---

Circle the idiom.

I'd like to live in the mountains someday.

Don't make a mountain out of a molehill.

The mountain peak looks as sharp as a knife.

---

Taj and Jayson _____ after the ice cream truck.

**followed      chased      went**

---

Place a ✓ by each antonym.

**brave**

❑ fearful

❑ loud

❑ tired

❑ mistaken

❑ patient

❑ cowardly

---

**The thought struck me** is an **idiom**. It shouldn't be taken literally.

Why might it make sense to say that a thought "strikes" someone?

_____

_____

_____

---

Write the suffix that can be added to each word.

use___ ___ ___

pain___ ___ ___

hope___ ___ ___

---

Name _____          **Week 33, Day 3**

My (dad, Dad) is taking me camping.

We (were, will be) leaving tomorrow.

---

Underline the word that has a prefix.

Mr. Reynolds gets impatient with my classmates

when they don't pay attention to his lessons.

---

Circle **S** for simile or **M** for metaphor.

The street was a river after the devastating storm.                  S          M

Kyle is a snake for playing such a nasty trick.                       S          M

Carmella is as quiet as a lamb when she wants to be.                 S          M

When he runs, he is as quick as lightning.                           S          M

Coach Pratt can be a bear when he's angry.                           S          M

Julia scrambled up the tree like a monkey.                           S          M

The sea is as blue as the sky.                                       S          M

---

Say the name of the picture. Write a polysyllable word that has the same vowel sound.

_____

---

Write three verbs using the future progressive tense.

_____

_____

_____

---

Circle the cause. Underline the effect.

The desert gets very little rain, so it

stays dry for most of the year.

---

Spell the word correctly.

**actuaully**

_____

---

Correct the title.

The New Puppys Collar

---

I cannot find my bag! I must have _____ it.

**misplaced          replaced          displaced**

---

Everyone should learn a sport. Sports are fun. Also, they are wonderful exercise. Playing sports is much better than staying inside. If you try a sport, you'll love it.

This paragraph mainly (gives details on a topic, describes the author's feelings).

Insert the missing comma.

I want to go outside to play so I better finish my homework.

Write a word that uses each pair of letters to make a **long e** sound.

**ie** _____          **ea** _____

**ee** _____          **ei** _____

Joe knows how to ride horses. _____, he knows how to milk cows.

**In addition**

**For example**

Maria gazed at the red bike shining in the window of Bob's Bike Shop. Then, she saw the price tag. "That's way too **expensive**!" she cried. Maria went to Morton's Bike Shop. Their bikes were just as nice, but they cost less.

What is the meaning of **expensive**? How do you know?

_____

_____

_____

_____

Complete the synonym.

**creep**

cr___w___

It can be hard to get people to recycle. Some people throw everything in the garbage. This isn't good for Earth.

If people learned more about recycling, they wouldn't throw everything in the trash. They'd understand how their actions affect the planet. In addition, cities and towns can help. They can place a recycling bin wherever there's a garbage bin. That way, people can throw everything where it belongs. These few steps can really help our planet.

What is the problem presented in the text?

_____

_____

What is one solution?

_____

_____

North America and Asia are examples of this three-syllable word.

c_____

Circle the words that relate to travel.

| habit | pause | journey |
|-------|-------|---------|
| voyage | atlas | experiment |
| cramp | sightsee | cabinet |

Synonyms (always, do not always) have the same exact meaning as each other.

Place a dot (•) between syllables.

n a t i o n a l

n a t u r e

n o n s e n s e

Place a ✓ by each prepositional phrase.

☐ **down the stairs**

☐ **near the car**

☐ **playing soccer**

☐ **make the bed**

☐ **around the corner**

☐ **quickly writing**

○ **creaky**

○ **criecky**

○ **creeky**

Circle the stronger sentence.

The horse jumped over the fence.

The horse leaped over the fence.

Underline the idioms. Then, choose one and explain what means.

I had to give a report in front of my class. I had mixed feelings about it. The topic was about baseball, which I really love. However, I usually get butterflies in my stomach when I have to stand up in front of a crowd. As it turns out, it was a piece of cake. Everyone loved my report, and I felt like I did a great job.

_____

_____

○ **sure**

○ **shore**

The **big black** cat jumped on the fence.

**correct order**        **incorrect order**

Correct the sentence.

I wanted to go to the fair but I had homework.

---

Complete the sentences with the correct relative pronouns.

The woman _____ lived next door

moved away.

A new family moved into her house,

_____was fun for the neighborhood.

---

Types of _____

---

Place a ✓ by each synonym.

**wee**

❑ little

❑ less

❑ tiny

❑ slight

❑ wide

❑ small

---

Circle the adage.

Stop and smell the roses.

Roses come in many colors.

I rose from my chair in a flash.

---

Gideon _____ at his little sister as she grabbed the last salty pretzel out of his hand.

**beamed     scowled     looked**

---

Place a ✓ by each antonym.

**wee**

❑ mammoth

❑ old

❑ huge

❑ great

❑ vast

❑ grow

---

**He wouldn´t give me the time of day** is an **idiom**. It shouldn´t be taken literally.

If someone won´t give you the time of day, what is he doing to you? Explain your answer.

_____

_____

_____

---

Write the suffix that can be added to each word.

collect___ ___ ___

direct___ ___ ___

act___ ___ ___

Yesterday, I rode (by, buy) the toy store on my bike.

I want to (by, buy) the jigsaw puzzle in the window.

---

Underline the word that has a prefix.

Suki could not go to band practice because she misplaced her flute.

---

Circle **P** for relative pronoun or **A** for relative adverb.

I will buy a baseball cap when we go shopping.                    **P        A**

I know who moved in next door yesterday.                          **P        A**

I cannot figure out where I left my shoes.                        **P        A**

I don't know whose car is in the driveway.                        **P        A**

I wonder why the overnight ski trip was canceled.                 **P        A**

I know which of the Lee sisters is older.                         **P        A**

I haven't decided to whom I will give the ticket.                 **P        A**

---

Say the name of the picture. Write a polysyllable word that has the same vowel sound.

_____

---

Write three coordinating conjunctions.

_____

_____

_____

---

Circle the cause. Underline the effect.

After eating too much, most people feel ill.

---

Spell the word correctly.

**voiyage**

_____

---

Correct the title.

Why Bears Shouldnt Sing

---

The **old nice** man is our neighbor.

**correct order          incorrect order**

I opened the basement door and then leaped back. Two green eyes stared at me from the darkness. The little creature said, "My name is Zork. Is this Planet Alpha?" I just shook my head, not able to speak and barely breathing.

This paragraph is (fiction/drama).

---

Write the sentence correctly.
ostriches are native to africa and can weigh up to 300 pounds.

_____

_____

---

Underline the word(s) with a **short u** sound.

I was amused by the cute chipmunk eating nuts.

---

First, Jen went apple

picking. _____,

she made apple cider.

**Then**

**Again**

---

Eden knocked over a jar of pickles. It broke on the supermarket floor. The store manager came over. "Who did this?" he said with a scowl. Eden could have lied, but she was **honest** and said that she knocked over the jar.

What is the meaning of **honest**? How do you know?

_____

_____

_____

_____

---

Complete the synonym.

**entire**

__h__ le

---

Underline an **idiom** that lets you know that the paragraph is comparing and contrasting two things. Then, write what the idiom means.

Maine and Florida are both popular states, but they don't have much in common. Maine gets a lot of snow and ice. It's very cold there in the winter. Florida, on the other hand, is very hot. People don't need to bundle up in the wintertime in Florida. In fact, people go there in the winter if they want to be warm. Nobody would go to Maine in search of sizzling heat!

_____

_____

---

This three-syllable word means to look at something carefully.

e_____

---

A (driveway, freeway, runway) is generally not a place for cars.

Place a dot (•) between syllables.

c a r n i v a l

c h a r c o a l

c l i m a t e

Place a ✓ by each simile.

☐ **She was as quick as a cat.**

☐ **She is a very kind person.**

☐ **She likes to play soccer.**

☐ **He had slept very late.**

☐ **He was jumping like a frog.**

Spell the word correctly.

**sweppt**

_____

Circle the stronger sentence.

My little brother is very naughty.

My little brother is not nice.

Underline the stage directions in the drama.

**Cody:** (pointing to a treasure chest on his front lawn) Where did that come from?

**Anil:** Beats me. Let's open it! (running for the treasure chest)

**Cody:** Anil, don't! We don't even know where it came from.

**Anil:** What could be wrong with opening a treasure chest? It has treasure inside!

**Cody:** (shaking his head) I don't know, Anil. I have a weird feeling about this.

**Anil:** I don't.

(**Anil** flings open the treasure chest as **Cody** takes a few steps back.)

○ **brake**

○ **break**

Aiden's _____ picked him up from school.

**Dad     dad**

Correct the sentence.

My homework was done so I went to Jamie's house.

Which sentences uses **who** as a relative pronoun?

❑ **The cat that lives across the street is really beautiful.**

❑ **Who could say it isn't?**

❑ **Frida asked me, "Who owns that cat?"**

❑ **I don't know the neighbors who own the cat.**

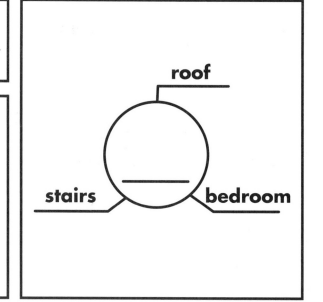

Place a ✓ by each synonym.

**record**

❑ **jot**

❑ **repeat**

❑ **word**

❑ **take down**

❑ **write**

❑ **print**

Circle the adage.

I am saving money for a bicycle.

Twenty nickels is equal to one dollar.

A penny saved is a penny earned.

Gabrielle _____ the kite's string as the wind got stronger.

**held      took      grasped**

Place a ✓ by each word with the vowel sound in **rain**.

❑ **banner**

❑ **undertake**

❑ **shameful**

❑ **Spanish**

❑ **fancy**

❑ **weights**

The students at Mills Primary School voted on their favorite subjects. While many students preferred art to science, math was by far the most popular subject at the school.

The graph (does, does not) support the statement above.

What other information does the graph provide?

_____

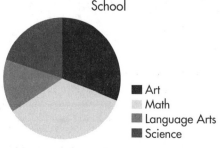

Favorite Subjects at Mills Elementary School

■ Art
  Math
  Language Arts
■ Science

Write the suffix that can be added to each word.

bright___ ___

hard___ ___

strength___ ___

We are going to the (sure, shore) this weekend.

I am (sure, shore) I will go swimming.

---

Underline the word that has a prefix.

Pedro rushed through his book report, so Ms. Cho made him rewrite it.

---

Circle **L** for literal or **F** for figurative.

| | | |
|---|---|---|
| Let's catch a movie on Saturday afternoon. | L | F |
| Line up outside the gym and get ready to run. | L | F |
| We slipped on the ice. | L | F |
| The school bell is way too loud. | L | F |
| My sister is always bugging me about taking her to the store. | L | F |
| We're working against the clock for the rest of the day. | L | F |
| I can't figure out the answer to the question. | L | F |

---

Say the name of the picture. Write a three-syllable word that has the same vowel sound.

_____

---

Write three suffixes.

_____

_____

_____

---

Circle the cause. Underline the effect.

After running, people may find

that their legs are sore and weak.

---

Complete the synonym.

**insist**

__em__ nd

---

Correct the title.

Millie, the Great Mesenger Dog

---

The **afternoon bright** sun beat down on us.

**correct order**          **incorrect order**

---

**Annie:** What's that? (bending down)

**Raul:** It's a baby bird. I think it's hurt.

**Annie:** (grabbing Raul's arm) Don't touch it. Let's get my mom. She can help.

The reader can tell this is a drama because (it has stage directions, it is written in stanzas).

---

Insert the missing comma.

Shirley dislikes social studies yet she always does well on the tests.

---

Underline the word(s) with a **long a** sound.

I asked them to weigh my pumpkin, and found out it was a whopping 50 pounds.

---

Jake doesn't like camping _____ he is afraid of bugs.

---

LaToya looked through the tent flap. She definitely saw **motion** out in the woods. Even though it was dark, she knew what she saw. Something had moved. Mom said there were no bears in Cove Park, but LaToya wasn't so sure.

What is the meaning of **motion**? How do you know?

_____  _____

_____  _____

_____  _____

_____  _____

---

○ **wringle**

○ **wrinckle**

○ **wrinkle**

---

**yet**

**because**

---

This three-syllable word names something that will help you look at the stars.

t_ _____

---

Sometimes, it can be hard to get all of your homework done. If this happens to you, just try these suggestions:

Keep a list of your assignments. When you complete one, cross it off. That way, you won't forget any assignments. Also, start your homework earlier, such as when you get home from school. You won't need to rush before going to bed. These simple steps can make a mountain of homework disappear more easily.

○ **chronology**

○ **comparison**

○ **cause/effect**

○ **problem/solution**

---

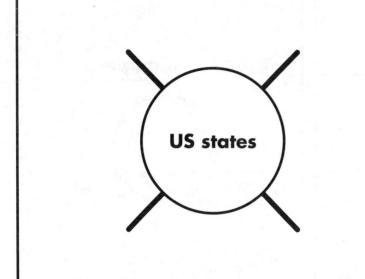

US states

**I am reading** is in the (present, future) progressive tense.

Place a dot (•) between syllables.

u n d e r s t a n d

u n h a p p y

u m b r e l l a

Place a ✓ by each idiom.

☐ **fish out of water**

☐ **see eye to eye**

☐ **hold your breath**

☐ **draw a blank**

☐ **answer the question**

☐ **blue as the sea**

Complete the antonym.

**soft**

sti___ ___

Circle the stronger sentence.

The water was only two feet deep.

The water was not deep.

Circle the misspelled words. Then, write them correctly.

   This was a terrific weekend. My cousin Hannah came to visit. Hannah is really funny. She told me these funny stories about a chimpanze and a crocadile she saw at the zoo. Then, my mom helped us do a science experament in the kitchen. Before Hannah left, we made sure she met all of my friends in my nayborhood. I can't wait until Hannah visits again.

_____        _____

_____        _____

◯ **piece**

◯ **peace**

The first answer _____ correct.

**isn't       ain't       aren't**

Correct the sentence.

I do not like peas nor do I like carrots.

---

Combine the sentences.

The researchers went to sea to record whale songs. They went last Tuesday.

_____

_____

_____

---

**maple**

apple            pine

---

Place a ✓ by each synonym.

**cruel**

☐ **naughty**

☐ **twirl**

☐ **wicked**

☐ **bend**

☐ **coil**

☐ **mean**

---

Circle the idiom.

Hold your horses!

The big bird bit the berry.

Do you like cats or dogs better?

---

Mrs. White wanted to give the class homework, but the students _____ her not to.

**persuaded      warned      commanded**

---

Place a ✓ by each antonym.

**cruel**

☐ **straight**

☐ **caring**

☐ **warm**

☐ **smart**

☐ **kind**

☐ **sad**

---

**I bite my tongue** is an **idiom**. It shouldn't be taken literally.

When might you "bite your tongue"?

_____

_____

_____

_____

---

Write the suffix that can be added to each word.

comfort___ ___ ___ ___

break___ ___ ___ ___

enjoy___ ___ ___ ___

We drove (over, above) the bridge.

Later, we drove (through, between) the woods.

---

Underline the word that has a prefix.

Although it's really unusual to see snow in Georgia, it has happened.

---

Circle **C** for correct or **I** for incorrect.

A play has a cast of characters.        C        I

Poetry sometimes rhymes.        C        I

A fiction story has stage directions.        C        I

A play has a setting.        C        I

A fiction story is about a real-world event.        C        I

Poetry is written in stanzas.        C        I

A fiction story can have dialogue.        C        I

---

Say the name of the picture. Write a polysyllable word that has the same vowel sound.

_____

---

Imagine you are writing your biography, and you have come to the events of this morning. Write a sentence to introduce the scene.

_____

_____

_____

_____

---

Circle the cause. Underline the effect.

The Amazon rain forest is being cut down, so people are trying to stop it.

---

Spell the word correctly.

**whillow**

_____

---

Correct the title.

The Two Ponies Wild Adventure

---

My sweater has **dull green** buttons.

**correct order**        **incorrect order**

Dylan Dray
danced all day.
He tripped on his toes
and fell on his nose.

The reader can tell this is poetry because (it tells a story/it rhymes).

---

Write the sentence correctly.

after you pass the museum, turn right onto the 12th street bridge.

_____

_____

---

Underline the word(s) with a **long e** sound.

When our test was complete, our teacher sent us out to the playground.

---

_____ she likes carrots, Milagros eats a lot of them.

**Because**

**Besides**

---

"I'll clean my room, walk Buck, and wash the dishes," Garrett told his mother. She didn't want him to camp out in Ramon's yard, but she looked like she was giving in. He had to think of something to **persuade** her.

What is the meaning of **persuade**? How do you know?

_____

_____

_____

_____

---

○ **toward**

○ **towred**

○ **toard**

---

   Benjamin Franklin invented many things. Believe it or not, he invented swim fins in 1717. In 1762, he made his own musical instrument. He named it the armonica. People touched their hands to curved glass pieces to make the notes. He later created a new kind of eyeglasses. They are called bifocals. Benjamin Franklin was a smart man who always thought about how to make life better.

What does the author want you to learn from this text?

_____

_____

_____

_____

_____

---

This three-syllable word names an animal that looks a lot like an alligator.

**c**_____

---

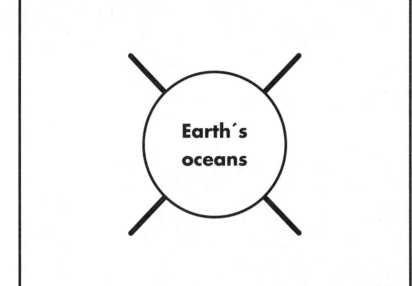

Earth's
oceans

**I was sleeping** is in the (present, past) progressive tense.

Place a dot (•) between syllables.

c o b b l e r

c o l l e c t

c o m m a n d

Place a ✓ by each simile.

☐ **She likes to swim.**

☐ **The glass looked like diamonds.**

☐ **I know he likes eating fruit.**

☐ **The cake was shaped like a football.**

☐ **He thinks he will like his teacher.**

◯ **carriage**

◯ **carrage**

◯ **carrige**

Circle the stronger sentence.

The car screeched to a halt.

The car came to a stop.

Circle the correct words.

My dad and I had a great time at the science museum yesterday. We got (to, too) do an experiment with static electricity. We also learned about Mars's (two, too) moons, Phobos and Deimos. After the museum, we each had a (piece, peace) of pie at our local bakery. It was a (grate, great) day.

We are planning another trip for next (weak, week). (There, Their) is a nice art museum only an hour away from our neighborhood. My dad says that it has a lot of paintings by a French artist called Monet. He is famous for a series of paintings he made of water-lily (pawns, ponds). As Monet grew older, his (eyesite, eyesight) became poor. As you can imagine, this changed his (stile, style).

◯ **ant**

◯ **aunt**

The cat is in the house, but the dog is in the yard.

**complete sentence**     **fragment**

Correct the sentence.

Will you play checkers or fly my kite Jen asked.

---

Complete the sentences with the correct relative pronouns.

I wonder _____ got the highest grade on the test.

He is the boy _____ dog we found yesterday.

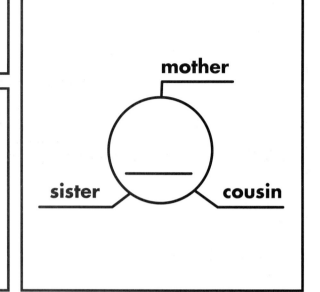

---

Place a ✓ by each synonym.

**explanation**

❒ sentence

❒ reply

❒ guess

❒ statement

❒ rethink

❒ answer

---

Circle the adage.

You should say you're sorry if you hurt someone.

I was sorry that I didn't study harder.

Better safe than sorry.

---

Shinji and Koji _____ their mother to take them to the movies, even though she wanted to stay home.

**coaxed       got       caused**

---

Place a ✓ by each antonym.

**explanation**

❒ song

❒ wonder

❒ question

❒ silence

❒ thanks

❒ problem

---

**I could do that standing on my head** is an **idiom**. It shouldn't be taken literally.

What do you think the idiom means?

_____

_____

_____

_____

---

Write the suffix that can be added to each word.

sick__ __ __ __

sad__ __ __ __

fair__ __ __ __

Do you know (whom, whose) fleece jacket this is?

I am wondering (who, whom) it belongs to so that I can return it.

---

Underline the word that has a prefix.

Finding the buried treasure was an amazing discovery.

---

Circle **S** for a sentence or **F** for a fragment.

| | | |
|---|---|---|
| Had off from school today. | S | F |
| My sister helps me with my homework. | S | F |
| Decided to go to Molly's house. | S | F |
| Juan sits behind me in class and talks too much. | S | F |
| Comes to visit every spring. | S | F |
| I found my grandma's diary in the basement. | S | F |
| Did not go to the fair. | S | F |

---

Say the name of the picture. Write a polysyllable word that has the same vowel sound.

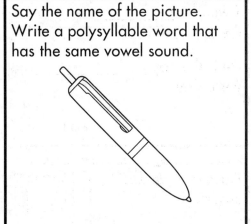

_____

---

Write three elements of fiction.

_____

_____

_____

---

Circle the cause. Underline the effect.

To become a doctor, you have to go to college.

---

Spell the word correctly.

**modeirn**

_____

---

Correct the title.

Dr Howell Helps Hanover

---

That **orange large** butterfly is called a monarch.

**correct order**          **incorrect order**

_____

We should go to the zoo for one of our class trips. We could learn a lot. We could learn about the animals we're already studying—and new ones too. Also, the zoo is really close by. We'd have a great time and learn a lot.

This paragraph is meant to (persuade the reader, inform the reader).

---

Insert the missing comma.

I love spending time with my cousins

but I hardly ever get to see them.

---

Circle the word(s) that rhyme with **prize**.
My disguise was a surprise. I was dressed as a clothesline! I had shirts and socks dangling from each arm. The pins didn't work though; the socks fell off twice!

---

Kimmy went to school,

the library, and the park.

_____, she

went home.

**However**

**Finally**

---

Guillermo listened carefully. He didn't hear a sound. There was only **silence**. Usually, his baby sister Marisa started crying at midnight. It was already 12:15 am, and she hadn't started yet.

What is the meaning of **silence**? How do you know?

_____

_____

_____

_____

---

Complete the synonym.

**nervous**

__ or__i__ d

---

There are many different types of paintings. Some paintings, called landscapes, are of places such as a city or a wide valley. Others may have much smaller subjects such as fruit or other household objects. Some painters like to paint people instead, whether in nature or the painter's own studio.

Paintings don't have to look like real life, however. Some paintings just show shapes such as squares and circles. Others are based on real-life subjects, but artists turn them into something that looks quite different. A painting can be anything the artist wants!

These paragraphs describe two different categories of paintings. What are they?

_____

_____

_____

---

This three-syllable word means "to pause."

**h**_____

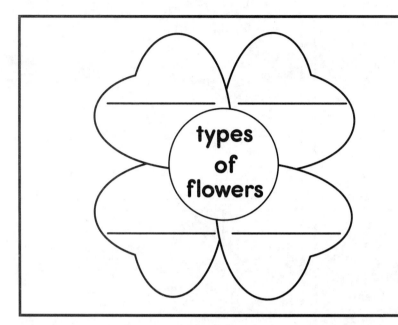

types
of
flowers

**I will be leaving** is in the (present, future) progressive tense.

Place a dot (•) between syllables.

e n g i n e e r

e n d u r a n c e

e x p e r i e n c e

Place a ✓ by each sentence that uses capital letters correctly.

❏ **I'll help Mrs. Ling.**
❏ **We will leave on sunday.**
❏ **She lives on Reed Street.**
❏ **My mother is a Doctor.**
❏ **I know how to speak french.**

Complete the synonym.

**sore**

p__ __n__u__

Circle the stronger sentence.

The cows grazed in the green pasture.

The cows ate grass outside.

Rewrite the paragraph using complete sentences.

   Exercise can make your heart, lungs, and bones healthy. It can really help you stay in shape. Goofing off in front of the TV can be. To stay in shape, playing a sport. You might find it fun. You might also new friends.

_____

_____

_____

_____

◯ **caret**

◯ **carrot**

Casey spent all afternoon on the **tele**phone.

**root word          prefix**

Fix the sentence.

My soccer game made me late  matt explained

Complete the paragraph by choosing the prepositions that fit best.

New neighbors moved (into, in) the house next door. Their dog barks (at, with) me every morning when I walk (for, to) the bus stop. It is either warning me to stay away (of, from) its house, or it wants to be friendly. Our dog barks when she hears someone walk (by, to) our house. If someone comes (at, to) the door, she is just excited to meet them!

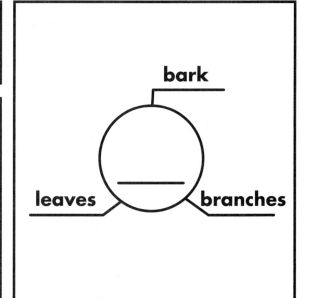

Place a ✓ by each synonym.

**accept**

❑ share

❑ allow

❑ understand

❑ give

❑ agree

❑ tell

Circle the idiom.

Cat got your tongue?

Her hair is longer than mine.

The ball almost hit me in the head!

Amber and Jane _____ a new ice cream flavor.

**designed    invented    made**

Place a ✓ by each antonym.

**accept**

❑ argue

❑ deny

❑ silence

❑ yell

❑ refuse

❑ disagree

The students in Mrs. Ferra's class voted on what to do for the school fund-raiser. Here are the results: Bake Sale—90%; Craft Sale—10%. Draw a pie chart showing the results.

Write a sentence to describe the results without referring to the numbers in your chart.

_____

_____

_____

_____

Find the suffix that can be added to all three words. Complete the words.

plan__ __ __ __

stop__ __ __ __

hug__ __ __ __

It has been a long time (after, since) I last saw Amy.

I hope she knows (why, where) to meet me.

---

Underline the word that has a prefix.

The class's behavior was a disgrace, and Mrs. Randall told them so.

---

Circle **S** for a sentence or **R** for a run-on.

| | | |
|---|---|---|
| We went to the party and had a good time. | S | R |
| My brother is home from college this week. | S | R |
| Sylvia didn't go I did. | S | R |
| Alejandra went to the store she bought milk. | S | R |
| When I come home from school, I have a snack. | S | R |
| Last week, I had a cold. | S | R |
| Don't run you'll fall. | S | R |

---

Say the name of the picture. Write a polysyllable word that has the same vowel sound.

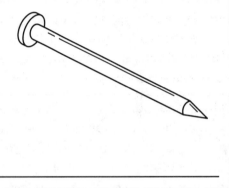

_____

---

Write three elements of drama.

_____

_____

_____

---

Circle the cause. Underline the effect.

It is cold in Colorado, so it gets a lot of snow in winter.

---

Spell the word correctly.

**sceinery**

_____

---

Correct the title.

Were Going to the Mountains

---

He has the **biggest striped** cat I've ever seen.

**correct order**          **incorrect order**

**167**

Carlos didn't want to go to Earth, but he had no choice. His mom's new job was in a place called Washington, DC. He didn't know what Earth would be like. He hoped there were fun things to do.

The reader can tell this paragraph is fiction because it (is written in verse, tells about an imaginary event).

---

Write the sentence correctly.

Jenna was exited to haves a window seet near the airplan's wing.

_____

_____

---

Circle the word(s) that rhyme with **ways**.

We won today's race! I was so happy with the result.

Actually, let me rephrase that. I was amazed!

---

Gina held Scruffy in the

bathtub _____

Theresa washed him.

**while**

**however**

---

Raj had studied every day for weeks. He could spell every word on the list backward and forward. He was ready. Raj knew he could **succeed**. He could beat all the other kids at the spelling bee.

What is the meaning of **succeed**? How do you know?

_____

_____

_____

_____

---

◯ **acshun**

◯ **action**

◯ **acktiun**

---

Flowers are beautiful, but they can be very fragile. They need certain things in just the right amounts to survive. Most flowering plants need plenty of sunlight in order to grow strong. Like animals, they also need water, though some plants need very little. Some people give their flowers plant food to help them grow. These things can make flowers healthy for the entire growing season. Too much of these things, however, can be just as bad as too little.

From the information in the text, do you think it is important to learn the needs of a certain type of flower before you plant it? Why or why not?

_____

_____

_____

_____

---

A piano and a guitar are examples of this three-syllable word.

**i**_____

---

Name _____  **Week 39, Day 1**

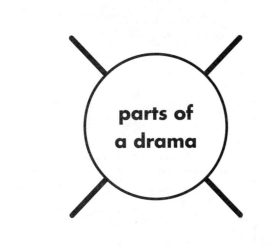

parts of a drama

My (two, too) brothers are going to the park.

What is an **autograph**?

_____

_____

_____

Place a ✓ by each four-syllable word

☐ **according**

☐ **bracelet**

☐ **disappointment**

☐ **explanation**

☐ **refrigerator**

☐ **improvement**

○ **realise**

○ **reelise**

○ **realize**

Circle the stronger sentence.

Anuja climbed the tree's old branches.

Anuja scaled the tree's crooked branches.

Rewrite the paragraph, correcting the run-on sentences.

   I have a book report due on Friday, I really need to get started on it. I read the book, but I just never got around to writing the report. If I don't go to Ming's house after school, I can work on it. Next time, I'll definitely start my report earlier, I promised myself I'll never let this happen again.

_____

_____

_____

○ **hole**

○ **whole**

Monday's test **slipped my mind**.

**prepositional phrase**     **idiom**

Correct the sentence.

john said is charlotte coming on saturday

Complete the sentences with the correct relative pronouns.

Can you show me the picture _____

won the art contest?

I also want to see the second-place winner,

_____ is said to be beautiful.

softball

swimming          _____          tennis

Place a ✓ by each synonym.

**experiment**

❑ try

❑ know

❑ wish

❑ explore

❑ understand

❑ test

Circle the adage.

Please try to be on time today.

Time flies when you're having fun.

I ran out of time to do all of my chores.

We watched as the chipmunk

_____ into the ground.

**moved     burrowed     went**

Place a ✓ by the prepositions.

❑ after

❑ who

❑ farther

❑ finally

❑ beneath

❑ surely

❑ in

Correct each sentence by adding a preposition.
The Carter family moved their new apartment.

_____

_____

Mrs. Rodriguez drove the state of Wyoming.

_____

_____

Write the suffix that can be added to each word.

tall___ ___ ___

great___ ___ ___

kind___ ___ ___

Did you give (him, to him) the message?

I'm afraid I haven't run (him, into him) yet.

---

Underline the word that has a prefix.

Leah got a high score on the test, even though she'd been uneasy about it.

---

Circle **S** for sentence or **F** for fragment.

You may go out to play now.          S     F

Going to the circus is fun.          S     F

After the game is over.          S     F

We dinner with Mel's family.          S     F

I like music a lot.          S     F

I my sister at college last week.          S     F

Be careful on the ice.          S     F

---

Say the name of the picture. Write a polysyllable word that has the same vowel sound.

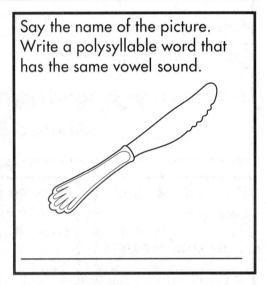

_____

---

Write three adjectives that describe your classroom.

_____

_____

_____

---

Circle the cause. Underline the effect.

When a baby starts to cry, it can be helpful to sing a lullaby.

---

Complete the antonym.

**raw**

_ oo_ _ _

---

Correct the title.

The Mistereous Mrs. Mills

---

My **new baby** sister's name is Gwen.

**correct order**          **incorrect order**

---

Lions are big cats. The lion is often called "The King of the Jungle." Lions live in Africa. Lions hunt other animals such as birds and zebras. Lions live together in groups called prides.

This paragraph is (fiction/nonfiction).

---

Insert the missing comma.

I will be going to the beach this weekend and I will also be going to the lake.

---

Correct the sentence.

I will love to go to the party tonight, but I have to go to a family dinner.

---

Grandma cooked dinner.

_____, Grandpa helped us with our homework.

**In the meantime**

**Even more**

---

Kamal scanned the ticket stub on the printer. He smiled as it popped up on the screen. He'd been great in the school play. This ticket would help Kamal remember this special night. Thanks to computers, he could **preserve** the image of the ticket forever, even though the play was over.

What is the meaning of **preserve**? How do you know?

_____

_____

_____

---

Spell the word correctly.

**purppose**

_____

---

Thomas Edison was born in Ohio in 1847. His family moved from Ohio to Michigan in 1854. By age 15, Edison had a job operating a telegraph.

Later, he went on to invent many famous items. Edison invented the phonograph in 1877. Just a few years later, he invented the lightbulb. In 1912, he designed a battery for a car called a Model T. Edison's great mind changed the world.

○ **chronology**

○ **comparison**

○ **cause/effect**

○ **problem/solution**

---

This five-syllable word names something that keeps food cold.

r_____

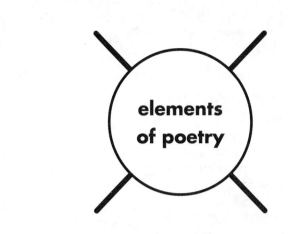

elements
of poetry

(Their, There) was a lot of rain

yesterday.

What does a **telegraph** do?

_____

_____

_____

Place a ✓ by each five-syllable word.

❑ **aquarium**

❑ **examination**

❑ **electricity**

❑ **handkerchief**

❑ **immediately**

❑ **persuade**

Complete the antonym.

**common**

___ ___re

Circle the stronger sentence.

The pony ate some grass.

The pony nibbled on a clump of grass.

Insert the correct punctuation.

   Neela and I had softball practice last weekend. As we were walking to the park, Neela shouted, "I don't have my glove" "Where did you leave it" I asked. At home, I guess. We raced back to Neela's house. As we walked inside, her mom was standing there with the glove in her hand. She was shaking her head but she was smiling. She's used to Neela forgetting things.

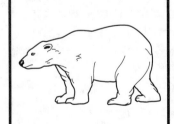

◯ **bare**

◯ **bear**

Juan's behavior was a **dis**grace.

**root word**        **prefix**

Correct the sentence.

on labor day I visited my grandma beth said

---

Complete the sentences with the correct relative pronouns.

The house _____ is next door is the

oldest one on the block.

I saw my sister talking to the boy

_____ house is painted green.

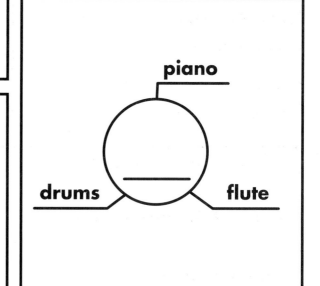

piano

drums      flute

---

Place a ✓ by each synonym.

**performed**

☐ show

☐ acted

☐ over

☐ lasted

☐ finished

☐ completed

---

Circle the idiom.

It's as cold as ice in here.

Strike while the iron is hot.

He is a very warm person.

---

I _____ my report in my bag, so it got wrinkled.

**tucked    jammed    placed**

---

Place a ✓ by each antonym.

**performed**

☐ tried

☐ incomplete

☐ followed

☐ rested

☐ unfinished

☐ untimed

---

→

figure of speech that compares two things
prefix meaning "not"
suffix meaning "someone who does a thing"
We got _____ the bus.

↓

a rest stop or hotel
modal auxiliary meaning "to have to"
We turned _____ a narrow alley.

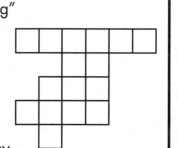

---

Write the suffix that can be added to each word.

delight___ ___ ___

wonder___ ___ ___

thank___ ___ ___

Name _____     **Week 40, Day 3**

(Can, May) you see through the grime on that window?

It (must, can) be cleaned because it's far too dirty to see anything.

---

Underline the word that has a prefix.

I lost my scarf yesterday, but it suddenly reappeared today.

---

Circle **C** for correct or **I** for incorrect.

| | | |
|---|---|---|
| A play includes stage directions. | C | I |
| Poetry is written in sentences. | C | I |
| A fiction story tells about imaginary events. | C | I |
| A play has dialogue. | C | I |
| A fiction story has a cast of characters at the beginning. | C | I |
| Poetry sometimes uses meter. | C | I |
| A play is written in verse. | C | I |

Say the name of the picture. Write a polysyllable word that has the same vowel sound.

_____

Write three adjectives that describe where you live.

_____

_____

_____

---

Circle the cause. Underline the effect.

Some trees lose their leaves when autumn comes.

---

Spell the word correctly.

**furnacse**

_____

---

Correct the title.

Our Bees and Wasps the Same

---

The **shiny silver** quarters are part of my coin collection.

**correct order**          **incorrect order**

The book's cover said "Do Not Open. Ever." Staring at the words, Kareena said to Jillian, "Well, it doesn't say we can't peek." A second later, the book started buzzing, almost like it heard what Kareena had said.

What does this paragraph have in common with a drama?

**Both have dialogue.     Both have meter.**

Write the sentence correctly.

the year had come to an end and we were all ready for a break

_____

_____

Underline the word(s) with a **long a** sound.

My Aunt Amy is away on vacation, and I'll be sad until she

gets back.

There are many

different breeds of dog.

_____, poodles

are one breed.

**In addition**

**For instance**

Billy ate a grilled cheese sandwich, an apple, and a cookie in a flash. Usually, he didn't eat so quickly, but he hadn't eaten since the game. After he'd **gobbled** everything in sight, he smiled and said, "So what's for dinner?"

What is the meaning of **gobble**? How do you know?

_____

_____

_____

_____

○ **presious**

○ **precious**

○ **presius**

Deserts don't get much rain. As a result, only certain plants live there. Cactuses thrive in deserts because they store large amounts of water inside themselves. When it does rain, cactuses soak up the water with their roots and keep it inside their stems. Cactuses are used to the dry conditions of the desert. They know what to do to survive.

What can you infer about plants such as lilies or mulberry trees that do not grow in deserts?

_____

_____

_____

_____

_____

This five-syllable word is an adverb that means "right now."

**i**_____

| | | | |
|---|---|---|---|
| discover | interchange | overreact | review |
| disable | interact | misjudge | recategorize |
| deprive | exhale | miscalculate | preview |
| dehydrate | exceed | midcycle | preseason |

- to become aware of
- to exchange two ideas or things
- to respond to something more forcibly than justified
- to look over again

- to put out of action
- to act upon each other
- to form a wrong opinion or conclusion
- to categorize again

- to deny the use or possession of something
- to breathe out
- to calculate wrong
- to look at before

- to lose a large amount of water
- to be better than or to go beyond the limit
- in the middle of a cycle
- before the season

| | | | |
|---|---|---|---|
| extension | honorable | sensible | wonderful |
| correction | harmless | liken | watchful |
| confusion | forgetful | invention | visible |
| attractive | flexible | imaginary | strengthen |

| | | | |
|---|---|---|---|
| the action or state of being extended | the act of correcting something | lack of understanding or state of uncertainty | having a pleasing appearance |
| worthy of honor | not likely to cause harm | likely not to remember | able to bend easily |
| having or showing good sense or judgment | to compare something to | something invented | not real |
| bringing wonder, delight, or pleasure | closely paying attention to | able to be seen | to make stronger |

# Answer Key

**Day 1**

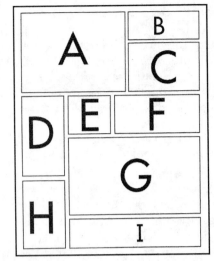

**Day 2**

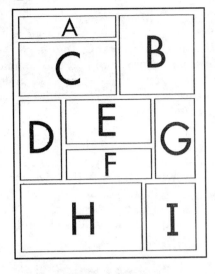

**Day 3**

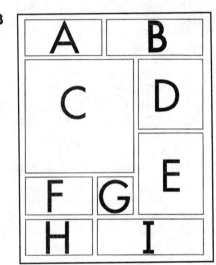

**Day 4**

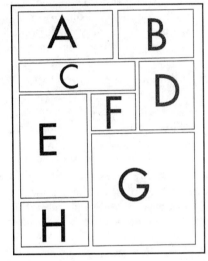

### Week 1, Day 1 (page 17)

A. He was surprised to meet two of his friends at the counter. They saw a movie together at the theater. Ben asked, "Are there any new movies out this week?" They decided to look online for showtimes. B. nouns; C. re•view, re•main•der, re•word; D. bouncy little puppy, new blue bicycle; E. rage; F. nouns: cab, curb, couple, cab, sidewalk, noise traffic, day; adjectives: yellow, dressed, crowded, deafening, ordinary; G. tired; H. weather; I. fragment

### Week 1, Day 2 (page 18)

A. "Don´t worry," she whispered. B. after the swim meet, under the umbrella; C. Every summer, welcomes many travelers to its parks and beaches. D. down, gloomy, unhappy; E. three; F. Mr. Lebowitz said, "Thank you for mowing my lawn, Javon." G. jolly, bright, joyful; H. present: have, spins, dream, is. past: went, typed, swam, kept; I. to work together

### Week 1, Day 3 (page 19)

A. luck, lucky; B. will happen; C. Was green and had thorns, just like a prickly plant. It was green and had thorns, just like a prickly plant. D. fragment; E. has/ have, think/thinks; F. Answers will vary. G. rare; H. A pear is a fruit. I. bad behavior

### Week 1, Day 4 (page 20)

A. be, is, was, is; B. delays, maze; C. complete sentence; D. Border collies are one of the most intelligent breeds of dogs in the world. E. James/him, I/me, everyone/them, she and I/us, she/her, Ohio/ it; F. beetle; G. Answers will vary. H. bad luck

### Week 2, Day 1 (page 21)

A. declarative, imperative, interrogative, exclamatory; B. do not always; C. west•ern, man•tel•piece, sis•ter•ly; D. Answers will vary. E. guest; F. We dug up a fossil! G. Answers will vary. H. true; I. Coming

# Answer Key

**Week 2, Day 2 (page 22)**
A. Have you ever been to North Carolina?
B. Check students' answers. C. The new town hall was too pricey and does not help the community.
D. bathe, clean, scrub; E. predicate; F. sentence;
G. stain, smear, foul; H. Across: theirs; Down: mine, ours; I. graceful

**Week 2, Day 3 (page 23)**
A. their, there; B. Four of my cousins; C. S, S, F, S, F, F, F; D. Down: who, whom; Across: which;
E. She was as sweet as pie. She was cold as ice to her friend. He ate like a pig at dinner. F. He, it, her;
G. glee; H. "Where are they going with that board?" Brook asked. I. spell incorrectly

**Week 2, Day 4 (page 24)**
A. tells a story; B. I ordered ham and eggs for breakfast this morning. C. must, will be;
D. sentence; E. It means they will not move. They are engaged in the play. F. A; kingdom;
G. Answers will vary. H. lead the wrong way

**Week 3, Day 1 (page 25)**
A. Answers will vary. B. joins; C. put in the wrong place; D. south dakota, new york, mississippi river;
E. lovely; F. warmly, happily, absently; G. I wanted to go to the racetrack, but it was closed for the season. Do you like vanilla cakes, or would you rather have chocolate with vanilla icing? H. bread;
I. compound sentence

**Week 3, Day 2 (page 26)**
A. fragment; B. The quick brown fox stopped suddenly. The shiny copper kettle whistled loudly from the stovetop. C. Jayden and I ran the cake up to the Morenos' apartment, and Sona brought the grab bags. D. pace, stroll, stride, hike; E. five; F. insert comma after "started"; G. she, he, I, it;
H. plural: sheers, tongues, fortunes, wolves; possessive: women's, baker's, Chris's, chief's; I. mix

**Week 3, Day 3 (page 27)**
A. she, it, her; B. shrieked; C. F, S, S, F, F, S, S;
D. lying, lay; E. cute, free, good, sharp; F. loaves, lives, chiefs; G. miles; H. on; I. misread

**Week 3, Day 4 (page 28)**
A. Answers will vary. B. Subject: Frogs; predicate: have different calls; C. I can't play. I have too much work to finish before class. D. subject; E. Too many cooks spoil the broth. F. stole; G. *tri-*, three, Answers will vary but may include triangle, triple, or tripod.
H. opposite

**Week 4, Day 1 (page 29)**
A. are driving, will be going, were planning, are buying; B. whose; C. mis•tak•en, mis•deed, mis•led;
D. At the grocery store. Salad instead. E. matter; F. The young woman leaned back on the metal bench waiting for the bus. G. Answers will vary. H. hear wrongly; I. direct object

**Week 4, Day 2 (page 30)**
A. "What a beautiful dog you have! What is his name, and may I pet him?" Carla asked her new neighbor. B. Answers will vary. C. a map for Townsend School and a map for Carter School;
D. scent, odor, reek, stench; E. Must; F. insert comma after "choir"; G. fountain, equator, oxen;
H. prey: a living creature hunted for food; scavenge: search; shallow: having a low depth; I. around, behind, among

**Week 4, Day 3 (page 31)**
A. howled; B. has dripped, is driving; C. S, C, C, S;
D. inside the box, under the pillow, behind the tree;
E. Run three times around the block! F. work very hard; G. scenery; H. abundant; I. below the ground

**Week 4, Day 4 (page 32)**
A. May, Will, should; B. they, Ali and Jack;
C. was, can; D. sunny, pour; E. Answers will vary but must address the adage. F. spying; G. a bird, to move from one region or land to another; ordinary, one section of Earth; H. lie beneath

**Week 5, Day 1 (page 33)**
A. He didn't get very many presents. The few he got, however, he loved. B. two, two; C. large•ly, bare•ly, care•ful•ly; D. we, I, you; E. amount; F. stormiest, most fun, most amusing; G. Answers will vary. H. fourth; I. on the

**Week 5, Day 2 (page 34)**
A. capitalize: mount, helens, Washington, lowercase: Volcano; B. Too many people working on a project can ruin the final product. C. A coordinating conjunction joins two sentences. Answers will vary.
D. chatter, speak; E. the plodding green turtle; F. will be; G. hush, keep quiet; H. correct: spices, crumbled, explorers, tryout; incorrect: trumpits, halte, allee, bluberr; I. to move unsteadily from side to side

**Week 5, Day 3 (page 35)**
A. Dr., doctor; B. cross out comma after Reggie;
C. Answers will vary. D. Across: where; Down: why, when; E. hard, mad, flat, solid (or any appropriate adjective); F. Answers will vary. G. geese;
H. in; I. not old enough

# Answer Key

## Week 5, Day 4 (page 36)
A. Fill in the blank. B. cause: They get a lot of sunlight. effect: Trees grow more quickly. C. am, will; D. Answers will vary. E. You can't teach an old dog new tricks. F. retreat; G. Answers will vary. H. fed too little

## Week 6, Day 1 (page 37)
A. Answers will vary. B. beginning; C. beneath the sea; D. Answers will vary. E. faint; F. Circle: but; Underline: I, Ben; G. group of trees; H. to many books; I. fragment

## Week 6, Day 2 (page 38)
A. My grandfather was a cowboy, and he used to ride a horse all day long. B. Answers will vary. C. Please return the tools you borrowed. D. beast, creature; E. whom; F. was; G. fielder; H. Adverb: carelessly, rally, early, frighteningly, dearly, ashamedly; Noun: ally, rally, bully; I. !

## Week 6, Day 3 (page 39)
A. her, hers; B. giggled, hilarious; C. main idea: Many words grow over time. supporting detail: Today, you can undermine more than walls. D. Snakeheads are dangerous fish because they do not have any natural enemies in US lakes and rivers. E. best or ideal; F. write hurriedly; G. blame; H. meanwhile; I. underdressed

## Week 6, Day 4 (page 40)
A. dark, dim, gloomy; B. "Does anyone here have the time?" asked Cole. "It's quarter past two," said Maggie. C. scampered; D. thundered; E. You can lead a horse to water, but you can't make him drink. F. imitate; G. Answers will vary. H. persuade

## Week 7, Day 1 (page 41)
A. am, are, is; B. There are too many onions on their pizza. C. un•der•arm, un•der•take, un•der•ly•ing; D. floor, barn, pony; E. settle; F. Ryan sprinted to the house. G. Answers will vary. H. peak; I. transition phrase

## Week 7, Day 2 (page 42)
A. am; B. was mapping, was daring, was asking, was raking, was fooling; C. am looking, are planning; D. stop, wait, rest; E. Will, are, will, be, being; F. left; G. criminal, pinning; H. Across: edge, knit, be; Down: rake, net; I. not complete

## Week 7, Day 3 (page 43)
A. leaves, boys'; B. dribbled, dunked; C. A, C, D; D. Across: fall, modern; Down: teacher, calm; E. a boat, a beaver; F. formal; G. dairy; H. knives; I. above your head

## Week 7, Day 4 (page 44)
A. protect, defend; B. Where will you be sitting at the dinner tonight? C. formal; D. ran quickly; E. Answers will vary but may include "out of nowhere" or "unexpected." F. feeling; G. Answers will vary. H. road that goes over another

## Week 8, Day 1 (page 45)
A. had, having, have; B. breath, breathing; C. wear•ing, nest•ing, stor•ing; D. doing, not; E. curious; F. A greater number of older residents were in favor of the law. G. Answers will vary. H. mail; I. helping verb

## Week 8, Day 2 (page 46)
A. which; B. Answers will vary. C. studying, gooding, collecktions; D. aid, relief, assist; E. the big blue house, the piping hot stove, the amazing flying squirrel, the majestic humpback whale; F. must; G. worsen, hurt; H. correct: maker, cover, kettle, robber; incorrect: blindefold, gluve, wildernes, lemmon. I., ?, , !

## Week 8, Day 3 (page 47)
A. began, saw; B. will be doing; C. Answers will vary. D. Across: appear, smooth; Down: best, hurt; E. night owl; F. wearing, using, putting; G. gaze; H. scythe; I. do too much

## Week 8, Day 4 (page 48)
A. swoop, stump, moccasin, pumpkin; B. What will you be painting for your art assignment? C. sharpening; D. a huge amount of snow falling down; E. There's no place like home. F. tunnel; G. Answers will vary. H. too ripe

## Week 9, Day 1 (page 49)
A. Answers will vary. B. adjectives; C. hurtling, barreling, sealing; D. *under-*, *mis-*, *tele-*, *im-*, *tri-* or *bi-*; E. ledge; F. pay too much; G. Answers will vary. H. always, running; I. prefix

## Week 9, Day 2 (page 50)
A. down a small hill, into a river, by the field, on a grassy knoll; B. fingers; C. If you wait too long to do something, you may miss the opportunity to do it. D. boiling, baking, sizzling; E. suffixes: *-graph, -ment, -ness, -tion,* prefixes: *dis-, tele-, pre-, under-, non-;* F. that; G. freezing, nippy, chilly; H. on topic; I. communication that is not understood

## Week 9, Day 3 (page 51)
A. Our, are; B. splattered; C. Answers will vary. D. Across: soldier, see; Down: wipe, trip; E. in order to, for instance, in addition to; F. handkerchief, mood; G. royal; H. between; I. overworked, oversleep

# Answer Key

## Week 9, Day 4 (page 52)
A. Answers will vary. B. Botswana, Angola, and Zambia are African countries. C. whom, will, be; D. completely confused about something; E. Don't judge a book by its cover. F. beak; G. Answers will vary. H. engineer

## Week 10, Day 1 (page 53)
A. "What flavor will you get?" Berry asked. "Oh, I don't know," I said. "What were you thinking of getting?" "I always get coconut," Berry replied, "but it looks like they're fresh out! It's a shame." B. readers; C. o•ver•pass, o•ver•cooked, o•ver•hang•ing; D. adjective; E.wheat; F. Ella hammered in the nail. G. Check students' answers. H. pole; I. simple sentence

## Week 10, Day 2 (page 54)
A. may; B. blubber, sob, wail, weep; C. to agree; D. upon, under, above; E. when someone moves about without making any noise; F. ,; G. plus, fusses; H. nouns: misdeed, misbehavior; verbs: misspell, underlie, overstep, overcook; adjectives: underwater, underneath; I. sky, cat, tree

## Week 10, Day 3 (page 55)
A. waiting, be; B. creaked loudly; C. before, for example, once, first, then, finally; D. Across: ornament, job; Down: woods, demand, disturb; E. Answers will vary but may include river, star, medicine, and peas. F. chew; G. worst; H. squawking grey goose; I. wrong, beneath, above

## Week 10, Day 4 (page 56)
A. Answers will vary. B. Circle: food fight incident; Underline: stricter cafeteria rules; C. During, of, under, was; D. to push against each something by the head; E. Something is very expensive. F. brook; G. Answers will vary. H. quote someone wrongly

## Week 11, Day 1 (page 57)
A. Answers will vary. B. theme; C. Answers will vary. D. Check students' answers. E. trimmed; F. "Good morning, Tran," Justine said. "I hoped to see you in class today. Ms. Sanchez would like us to split up into reading groups, and I would like you to be in mine." G. Check students' answers. H. made, barely; I. won't

## Week 11, Day 2 (page 58)
A. !; B. Answers will vary. C. the sun; D. spot, discern, glimpse; E. to feel out of place; F. am; G. her, us, you, it, them; H. wordy, "talk your ear off," talks too much; I. to not understand something

## Week 11, Day 3 (page 59)
A. Two, to, too; B. popped, snapped; C. Answers will vary. D. Before Michigan was admitted to the United States, it had been a separate territory for about thirty years. E. under, across, against, through, around (or any appropriate prepositions; F. talk speedily; G. blend; H. gleam; I. not complete

## Week 11, Day 4 (page 60)
A. thrilled, delighted; B. I was going to ask her, but she had already left. C. whose, is; D. rough feeling; E. Good things come to those that wait. F. forgive; G. Has, having, having, have, has, have, have; H. not perfect

## Week 12, Day 1 (page 61)
A. fragments: Norwegians, Swedes, and Germans also; run-ons: During the Great Famine, a number of Irish citizens came hoping for prosperity, they were not the only ones coming at the time. B. ?; C. im•med•i•ate, im•press, im•pa•tient; D. -ment, -er, -or, -ness, -en; E. excited; F. must, can, May; G. wildlife, habitat, endangered, conservation, extinction; H. paws; I. come

## Week 12, Day 2 (page 62)
A. was; B. Answers will vary. C. on top of the world; D. call out, wail, cry, roar; E. whispered; F. will be; G. will, can, might; H. Answers will vary. I. too

## Week 12, Day 3 (page 63)
A. There's, theirs; B. difficult, easier; C. Answers will vary. D. over the moon; E. erupt; F. There is, I have; G. howl; H. not obey; I. waltz

## Week 12, Day 4 (page 64)
A. can; B. Thanks, guys; C. red, that; D. speaking to a knowledgeable person for advice; E. Beauty is in the eye of the beholder. F. Answers will vary. G. gallon; H. give up

## Week 13, Day 1 (page 65)
A. run-ons: Three families lived in the old Bilby house, one lived on each floor. On the ground floor, the Rios family kept mostly to themselves, they spent most weekends out in the state park. fragments: In the attic, crammed in under a slanting roof, the Miller family. B. secondhand; C. not trust; D. was reading, am reading, will be reading; E. improve; F. Check students' answers. G. move: glide, hustle; speak: utter, declare, bellow, mutter; study: review, cram, inspect; H. false; I. main verb

# Answer Key

## Week 13, Day 2 (page 66)
A. am; B. Answers will vary. C. informative; D. overdue, delayed; E. Miss Schwartz asked, "How was your trip to Hawaii?" F. capturing; G. early, too soon; H. narrative; I. relieved, reopened

## Week 13, Day 3 (page 67)
A. are sharing, are starring; B. That sharp kitchen knife is used to chop vegetables. C. a tiger lying peacefully under a maple tree; D. lost in thought; E. caboose, railroad tracks, engine, conductor; F. snows now; G. oxen; H. reindeer; I. not happy

## Week 13, Day 4 (page 68)
A. Answers will vary. B. Could you drive me there, or is it too late? C. ,; D. recognition; E. Stop fooling with me. F. fierce; G. Answers will vary. H. polar

## Week 14, Day 1 (page 69)
A. Examples: business letter, giving a speech, talking to a teacher or principal, writing an essay; B. evidence; C. trou•ble, squab•ble, un•a•ble; D. Check students' answers. E. bring; F. "Hey Tommy," Juanita called out. "Are you going to enter a project in the science fair this year? Do you need a partner? If so, I think I have some good ideas for an experiment." G. Answers will vary. H. hotel, improve, jealous, onion, medal; I. helping verb

## Week 14, Day 2 (page 70)
A. will be; B. A watched pot never boils. C. A stitch in time saves nine. D. cut short, knock off, shut down, end; E. beneath, before, behind; F. Many people have taken ferries down the Mississippi River. G. begin, initiate, take up; H. Pluto, orbit, satellites, craters, asteroids; I. to, to

## Week 14, Day 3 (page 71)
A. stairs, stares; B. The waving school flag flapped in the wind. C. Answers will vary. D. under the weather; E. over, through, under, across; F. will, have, will; G. urge; Answers will vary. H. gurgling baby boy; I. two feet

## Week 14, Day 4 (page 72)
A. of the eyes or lenses; B. The peaches were growing soft when we picked them. C. —, that, !; D. showed; E. Our class field trip was to Mount Rushmore, which is a sculpture carved on the side of a mountain of George Washington, Thomas Jefferson, Abraham Lincoln, and Theodore Roosevelt. F. couple; G. For decades, Then, because, However, First, so, Most importantly; Answers will vary. H. tomato

## Week 15, Day 1 (page 73)
A. where, why, when; B. when; C. when; D. skip, waddle, scamper; E. mistake; F. Answers will vary. G. Because, also, For example, Then; H. hanger; I. relative adverb

## Week 15, Day 2 (page 74)
A. can; B. opinion; C. While, In order to, Instead of, Although; D. purr, buzz; E. where, why; F. ,; G. should, shall, is; H. verbs: displace, distrust, disowned; adjectives: inactive, disagreeable, improper, impatient, disowned; I. they're

## Week 15, Day 3 (page 75)
A. who, them; B. Darnell heard musical wind chimes tinkling from next door. C. Answers will vary. D. lucky in love; E. Check students' answers. F. Examples: happily, luckily, honestly, truly; G. gaze; H. Where would you find Arkansas on a map of the United States? I. three colors

## Week 15, Day 4 (page 76)
A. foot; B. helping: can, will be, should, can; main: meet, running, wait, work; C. Margaret studied her notes and said, "I think I need to do more research on my topic [because] I need more facts to support my ideas." D. a royal leader; E. Got information from a direct source; F. peace; G. Answers will vary but should include two relative adverbs. H. hurricane

## Week 16, Day 1 (page 77)
A. why, when, where; It changes what you want to learn about the Thomas family going away. B. able; C. care•less, blame•less, fear•less; D. it, where; E. dairy; F. Katie got a new puppy. G. Answers will vary. H. throne; I. simple past

## Week 16, Day 2 (page 78)
A. must; B. narrative; C. why, when; D. unwell, bedridden, sick; E. to not stir up trouble; F. ?; G. healthy, well; H. Answers will vary. I. there

## Week 16, Day 3 (page 79)
A. why, when; B. Rosario is interested in learning about different saltwater fish. C. Answers will vary. D. in between the lines; E. Enrico is sound asleep. F. when; G. free; H. will be; I. four

## Week 16, Day 4 (page 80)
A. four times your size; B. Marta said that it would hail, but it never did. C. The Lincoln Memorial is one of the most popular monuments in Washington, DC, perhaps because Lincoln himself was such a popular president. D. stressed and tired; E. You need to make up your mind about what you want to do. F. island; G. Answers will vary. H. over, behind, around

# Answer Key

## Week 17, Day 1 (page 81)
A. -er, -ness, -tion; B. verbs; C. fright•en, hap•pens, in•tense; D. true; E. electric; F. Valerie called out to her best friend, "Wait up!" "What is it?" Rebekah asked. "You have been elected class president," Valerie answered. G. Answers will vary. H. Answers will vary. I. linking phrase

## Week 17, Day 2 (page 82)
A. in circles, around the ice rink; B. Answers will vary. C. informative; D. drizzle, shower, cloudburst; E. was, will be, is; F. !; G. which, who, whose; H. Answers will vary. I. Their

## Week 17, Day 3 (page 83)
A. quietly, when, quickly; B. white garage; C. Answers will vary. D. Don´t worry it is not a big deal. E. they´re, their, there; F. turn suddenly; G. crumb; H. will be; I. with no ending

## Week 17, Day 4 (page 84)
A. Fill in the last blank. B. Hector is wondering where to put the goalposts. C. Thomas Nast was a famous cartoonist whose drawings once helped capture a thief. D. stood close by; E. Do not believe everything you are told. F. shift; G. You should introduce your topic and state your opinion early. This makes it clear to the reader what you are writing about and what opinion you hold. H. words that make no sense

## Week 18, Day 1 (page 85)
A. should, will, ought, might, must, could; B. end; C. because, that, For example; D. grumble, mutter, whisper; E. behaved; F. nor, for; G. Answers will vary. H. vane; I. vain

## Week 18, Day 2 (page 86)
A. on a farm, by a beautiful mountain, in the country; B. as light as a feather, as pretty as a picture, as happy as a clam; C. informative; D. soar, glide; E. Mother packed the picnic basket with salad, sandwiches, fruit, and water. F. "Class," Mr. Hopper said, "I would like you to write a report about Dr. Martin Luther King Jr., who was a great leader." G. cider, skylight, confide; H. Answers will vary. I. wear

## Week 18, Day 3 (page 87)
A. when, unless; B. will be, am; C. a weakness; D. anxious, bored, cheerful, jealous; E. Quentin exclaimed, "I couldn´t believe how spectacular the Grand Canyon is! Have you ever been there?" F. whose, Could, would; G. rally; H. necessary; I. someone who writes

## Week 18, Day 4 (page 88)
A. whose, Answers will vary; B. Mr. Dalliard, who lives next door, jogs and sings each morning. C. am, can; D. a quick look; E. something very easy to do; F. alert; G. Answers will vary. H. looks for clues

## Week 19, Day 1 (page 89)
A. Underline: martin, germany, martin, english, german, spanish, german; Circle: Friend, Languages, Today, Teach, Ten; B. noun phrase; C. writ•er, ci•der, hap•pi•er; D. !; E. waste; E. Dr. Wilson asked, "Where do you think Skip hurt himself, Amber?" "On his paw," Amber answered. "Skip tripped while running. Will he be OK?" "He will be fine with rest," Dr. Wilson said. F–G. Answers will vary. H. cupboard, phone, relief; I. Do

## Week 19, Day 2 (page 90)
A. dictionery, meens; B. The early bird gets the worm. C. informative; D. prune, truthful, tuning; E. metaphor; F. ought; G. tired, solid, merry; H. metaphors: drowning in tears, mirroring her actions, a walking dictionary; similes: gentle as a lamb, hungry as a horse, swift as a deer; I. Where

## Week 19, Day 3 (page 91)
A. can, is; B. Gina adopted a young border collie from the animal shelter. C. Answers will vary. D. crouch, hunch, slump, squat; E. Her voice was pleasing. F. treasure dearly; G. whose; H. will; I. plays the piano

## Week 19, Day 4 (page 92)
A. treasure, cherish; B. The sun shone through the curtains, and the birds burst into song. C. rumbled; D. people who live in a particular place for a long period of time; E. teeth, works with teeth; F. onion; G. Answers will vary. H. awkward

## Week 20, Day 1 (page 93)
A. and, but, so; B. Mr. Ito, my teacher, smiled and said, "Class, you are an amazing group of students!" (period as end punctuation acceptable as well); C. cows, crops, chickens, tractor, horses; D. mr. wang, north pole, south america, mount everest; E. dragon; F. but, so; G. Answers will vary. H. grade, grumble, design, icy, glow; I. adjective

## Week 20, Day 2 (page 94)
A. , so; B. Be careful of your actions, because someone will usually see you. C. informative; D. guide, head, steer; E. whom; F. Because; G. trail, go behind, follow; H. Answers will vary. I. its

# Answer Key

**Week 20, Day 3 (page 95)**
A. might, would, ought; B. "Did you hear that Justin sprained his ankle yesterday, so he will not be able to run in the next track meet?" Allen asked Mr. Barnett, his gym teacher. C. Answers will vary. D. echo, honk, jingle, screech; E. Look before you leap. F. Examples: studied, left; G. lair; H. —, !; I. struggled

**Week 20, Day 4 (page 96)**
A. Answers will vary. B. "How on Earth did you find them?" said Carter. C. crouched, pounced; D. someone who controls a machine; E. smart about things; F. remain; G. hatter, lawyer, reader, Southerner, islander; H. brownie

**Week 21, Day 1 (page 97)**
A. !, ?, —; B. who; C. sto•ry, nar•ra•tive, dra•ma; D. Check students' answers. E. accuse; F. washington, dc, lincoln memorial, washington monument, united states; G. She was very cheerful. H. creek; I. who

**Week 21, Day 2 (page 98)**
A. where; B. under the gate, into the backyard, on the grass, across the ground, between a fence post and the gate, on its side; C. metaphors: whiter than snow, hotter than an oven, floating on air; similes: proud as a peacock, cold as ice, fit as a fiddle; D. floor, book, tale; E. The old gray mare is still not what she used to be. F. should; G. narrative, poem, play; H. Answers will vary. I. It's

**Week 21, Day 3 (page 99)**
A. meeting, meats; B. wrinkled, scratched; C. A, D; D. jiggle, squirm, twist, wiggle; E. train; F. Answers will vary. G. area; H. up, which; I. can be fixed

**Week 21, Day 4 (page 100)**
A. "Another problem," Chen sighed, "is that we do not have enough teammates, and we need at least two more people to play against the West Somerset Wildcats." B. Paul, Brooke; C. shot, scrambled; D. a surplus of money; E. got the answer right; F. solid; G. Answers will vary. H. can be moved

**Week 22, Day 1 (page 101)**
A. Examples: *mis-, dis-, over-, under-, re-, un-, in-, im-*; B. editing; C. can be done; D. Answers will vary. E. slope; F. of, under/between/around/behind, at; G. Answers will vary. H. admit, alligator, ancestor, anchor, astronaut; I. possessive pronoun

**Week 22, Day 2 (page 102)**
A. who; B. relative pronouns: who, which; relative adverbs: where, when; C. Answers will vary.
D. donate, hand over, lend; E. must; F. Jenna loved to listen to the songs from an old musical called *My Fair Lady*. G. get, take, hold onto, receive, keep; H. Answers will vary. I. Your

**Week 22, Day 3 (page 103)**
A. me, herself; B. That old washing machine still works very well. C. Answers will vary. D. mumble, murmur, mutter, whisper; E. worn out; F. long /i/ sound; G. usual; H. whom; I. invisible

**Week 22, Day 4 (page 104)**
A. Check students' answers. B. I won't start the engine until everyone is in the car. C. twinkled; D. a place where people must stay to prevent the spread of illness; E. lost an opportunity; F. burst; G. Answers will vary. H. birch

**Week 23, Day 1 (page 105)**
A. Answers will vary. B. fragment; C. 4, 2, 3, 1; D. scamper, gallop, bolt; E. intend; F. cooking, chopped, roasted, shredded, baked; G. Answers will vary; H. sew; I. children's

**Week 23, Day 2 (page 106)**
A. whom; B. in the conclusion; C. Astronauts, space, simulator, chamber, spaceship, outer space; D. dazzling, shiny; E. The shiny copper kettle is on the stove; F. will; G. shady, dark, dull; H. Answers will vary. I. You're

**Week 23, Day 3 (page 107)**
A. that, his, It; B. was, will be; C. F, L, L, L, F, F, L; D. bellow, cry, scream, screech; E. when, where; F. a second best idea; G. scale; H. whose; I. to make simple

**Week 23, Day 4 (page 108)**
A. check, test; B. Ray has a new mower, which he keeps in the shed. C. new basketball; D. a public showing of items, usually artwork; E. staying up late; F. visible; G. B, C, E; H. make someone scared

**Week 24, Day 1 (page 109)**
A. *non-, over-, bi-*; B. imperfect; C. We'll deal with that problem when it happens. D. Check students' answers. E. lucky; F. around, over, on; G. Answers will vary. H. crumb, freckle, explore; I. uncle

**Week 24, Day 2 (page 110)**
A. whose; B. plus, First, Then, Next, Finally; C. the history of fishing in the United States; D. sprouted, sprung up; E. will be, am, was; F. who; G. posted, toasting; H. Don't put all of your eggs in one basket. I. Weigh

# Answer Key

**Week 24, Day 3 (page 111)**
A. adjustable; B. "Today," Mr. Humphries said, "a marine biologist will talk about whales in the Pacific Ocean." C. Answers will vary. D. was, will be; E. as stubborn as a mule; F. Answers will vary. G. thumb; H. North Dakota; thumb; I. to make tender

**Week 24, Day 4 (page 112)**
A. Answers will vary. B. "Does anyone here have the time?" asked Cole. C. My older sister, Leshawna, who loves history and English, will be starting at Middlebury High School next year. D. diamonds; E. It's your decision; F. mermaid; G. turn, memory; Answers will vary. H. chimpanzee

**Week 25, Day 1 (page 113)**
A. Answers will vary. B. have opposite; C. high; D. In addition, For example, However, Also; E. twelfth; F. slower, slowest; better, best; worse, worst; G. After, on, up, on, through, in, of, around, to; H. lead; I. incorrect order

**Week 25, Day 2 (page 114)**
A. "Stop!" she screamed. B. seasons; C. which; D. kind, soft; E. It was raining cats and dogs. F. shrieked; G. rough, harsh; H. The graph tells how many of the 46 pencils each of the four students sold. I. -ful

**Week 25, Day 3 (page 115)**
A. that, when; B. dislike; C. S, S, M, M, S, M, S; D. Answers will vary. E. Answers will vary but may include above, across, after, alongside, and among. F. cause: They hear a storm coming. effect: Animals seek shelter. G. bulge; H. The Astronaut Goes to the Moon; I. correct order

**Week 25, Day 4 (page 116)**
A. teaches about a place; B. I enjoy playing field hockey, but I don't have time anymore. C. great, state, yesterday; D. For example; E. happy. Monique hums and smiles. F. signal; G. problem/solution; H. language

**Week 26, Day 1 (page 117)**
A. Examples include shout, cry, cry out, howl, and wail. B. beginning; C. grate•ful, fan•ci•ful, pow•er•ful; D. shriek, sneeze, sneak; E. moist; F. Trevor flew down the stairs. G. won't, I'm, Let's, we're; will not, I am, Let us, we are. H. mane; I. simile

**Week 26, Day 2 (page 118)**
A. "Are you going to the play?" she asked. B. birds; C. whom, that, who, which; D. order, rule; E. I had a change of heart. F. declared; G. answer, ask; H. No. Jayne only read one more book than Marcella. I. -ly

**Week 26, Day 3 (page 119)**
A. heel, heal; B. impossible; C. S, S, F, S, F, F, F; D. Examples include straightening, unfaithful, and repaying. E. Answers will vary. F. cause: People who eat properly; effect: often stay healthy; G. obey; H. Mrs. Gordon's Garden; I. faraway sound

**Week 26, Day 4 (page 120)**
A. tells a story; B. read, red; C. family, stream; D. In addition; E. cried or shouted. Mr. Behr is shouting and upset. F. glaring; G. a note or writing sent over a long distance; H. shallow

**Week 27, Day 1 (page 121)**
A. Answers will vary. B. simile; C. fro•zen, fig•ure, flut•tered; D. tough, shove, bud; E. range; F. Javier poked his finger in the pie. G. celabrated (celebrated), poring (pouring)Naturaly (Naturally), umbrela (umbrella), retreeted (retreated), newsance (nuisance); H. muscle; I. modern

**Week 27, Day 2 (page 122)**
A. "We're going to be late," Emma said. B. US states; C. what/which/whose, which, who, whom; D. low, hushed, soft, whisper; E. Jane has a shot at the blue ribbon. F. exclaimed; G. noisy, loud; H. It shows how much more money Hector and LaTasha earned than Amelia and Randy. I. -ness

**Week 27, Day 3 (page 123)**
A. In, onto; B. incorrect; C. C, C, C, I, I, C, I, C; D–E. Answers will vary. F. planet; G. dull; H. Tom's Terrible Tomatoes; I. correct order

**Week 27, Day 4 (page 124)**
A. tells a story; B. bear, bear, bares; C. tried; D. Therefore; E. ruined or wrecked. The materials of the project were scattered on the ground. F. service; G. cause/effect; H. photographer

**Week 28, Day 1 (page 125)**
A. Examples include happy, joyous, gleeful, and merry. B. stanzas; C. travels to the stars, looks at and studies the stars; D. protection, national; E. colony; F. Jasmine raced through the park. G. I (eye), to (too), pail (pale), so (sew), There (their), here (hear); H. doe; I. fraction

# Answer Key

## Week 28, Day 2 (page 126)
A. "Do you want to come to my house?" Todd asked.
B. flowers; C. whom, which; D. feel, think, guess,
sense; E. Don't judge a book by its cover. F. tore;
G. with, behind, across, during; H. No. Soccer is the
most popular sport, while hockey is
the least popular. I. -es

## Week 28, Day 3 (page 127)
A. in, along; B. misbehaves; C. F, S, F, S, F, S,
F; D–E. Answers will vary. F. effect: People can
catch colds. cause: If they do not bundle up in cold
weather; G. relief; H. Pluto, the Dwarf Planet;
I. correct

## Week 28, Day 4 (page 128)
A. teaches about an animal; B. it's, to; C. rowed,
boat, shore; D. As a result; E. a book written about
someone's life, writes a book about someone's life;
F. smooth; G. problem/solution; H. invent

## Week 29, Day 1 (page 129)
A. Answers will vary. B. dialogue; C. through•out,
dur•ing, af•ter•ward; D. huge, enormous, giant;
E. nonsense; F. Hoshi gazed at the stars;
G. Saturday, Uncle, Toby, Texas, Spotty, Mom, I;
H. moose; I. sometimes true

## Week 29, Day 2 (page 130)
A. "Are you bringing brownies?" Sarah asked.
B. Earth's oceans; C. who, that; D. dash, hurry, race,
bolt; E. Two wrongs don't make a right. F. cracked;
G. delay, wait; H. Answers will vary. I. -ning,
-ging, -ting

## Week 29, Day 3 (page 131)
A. than, then; B. preparations; C. a note made after
writing; D. Answers will vary. E. up, under, until;
F. cause: When winter comes; effect: it snows;
G. grip; H. How to Succeed in Writing;
I. incorrect order

## Week 29, Day 4 (page 132)
A. teaches about tulips; B. I do not like basketball,
nor do I like football. I like baseball, but no one else
in my family does. C. Do, you, to; D. in a script;
E. action, The passage shows Jaden taking action to
help Mr. Walker. F. castle; G. comparison;
H. quarrel

## Week 30, Day 1 (page 133)
A. numb, glacier, subzero, bitter; B. prose, poetry;
C. te•le•graph, au•to•graph- bi•og•ra•phy;
D. September, Monday, Florida; E. voice; F. Patrick
eyed the pie on the counter. G. She and I like to my
house after school. (She and I like to go to my house

after school.) Other times we trees. (Other times
we climb trees.) I'm really glad that Betsy my best
friend. (I'm really glad that Betsy is my best friend.)
H. fourth; I. After

## Week 30, Day 2 (page 134)
A. "We won the game!" Javier exclaimed. B. bodies
of water; C. when, why, why, when, when; D. worn,
aged; E. The early bird gets the worm. F. pranced;
G. recent, latest, modern, current; H. bustling, dully,
warm; Answers will vary. I. -y

## Week 30, Day 3 (page 135)
A, who, who; B. remove; C. S, R, S, R, R, S, R;
D. Examples include existed, Mississippi, and
peppermint. E. Answers will vary. F. effect: People stay
in shape. cause: when they get a lot of exercise;
G. sneak; H. The Bear and Her Cubs; I. incorrect order

## Week 30, Day 4 (page 136)
A. tells a story about a trip; B. "Yes," Kyra agreed,
"we'll camp out in the morning." C. Patches, cat,
back; D. Then; E. Looking around or searching;
Curtis looks around the boxes, under the stairs, and
in old books. F. soldier; G. chronology;
H. remember

## Week 31, Day 1 (page 137)
A. Answers will vary. B. point of view;
C. par•tic•u•lar; pro•nounce, pro•tec•tion;
D. mother, student, math; E. service; F. Lucinda
dashed toward the school bus. G. I really like
reading books they can take you to places you can't
go in real life. (I really like reading books because
they can take you to places you can't go to in real
life.) For example, you can go to other planets
you can go back in time or to other countries. (For
example, you can go to other planets. You can also
go back in time or to other countries.) H. weight;
I. during

## Week 31, Day 2 (page 138)
A. My school, Lee Elementary School, is on Main
Street. B. school subjects; C. which, which; D. close
by; E. Two heads are better than one. F. sneaked;
G. far off, distant, a long way; H. increased; I. -ment

## Week 31, Day 3 (page 139)
A. may, can; B. unfair; C. Mel probably wouldn't be
able to understand what Tony was trying to tell her.
To her, he might look like he was going mad. Maybe,
she would think there had been a disaster! D–E.
Answers will vary. F. effect: Children do not do well
in school. cause: if they stay up too late; G. shout;
H. The Three Branches of Government;
I. incorrect order

# Answer Key

## Week 31, Day 4 (page 140)
A. gives details on a topic; B. first, third; C. We, jelly, we; D. Now; E. *bi-* (two), *tri-* (three), *quad-* (four), *mis-* (wrongly), *non-* (not), *under-* (too little); F. Main St. G. It is informative. The author states simple facts about events in Washington's life. H. fortunate

## Week 32, Day 1 (page 141)
A. consider, wonder, reflect, review; B. Do you want to go swimming, or would you rather go on a picnic? C. set•ting, char•ac•ter, e•vent; D. won't, shouldn't, I'm; E. cabbage; F. Lilly dangled the yarn in front of the cat. G. For example, we grow roses, daisies, and tulips. In addition, we grow tomatoes. On the weekend, Dad and my sister do the weeding. Gardens can be a lot of fun, but they are also a lot of hard work. H. warn; I. metaphor

## Week 32, Day 2 (page 142)
A. My cousin Helen is going to New York City on Friday. B. vegetables; C. that, whose, which, that; D. lay out, sketch, plot, design; E. Don't count your chickens before they're hatched. F. planted; G. whose, that, which; H. Students should write a brief paragraph that introduces an informational topic. I. *-hood*

## Week 32, Day 3 (page 143)
A. except, accept; B. disappeared; C. M, S, M, M, S, M, S; D. Answers will vary. E. informative; F. cause: The sport rugby was invented in England. effect: Then, it started being played in other countries. G. shallow; H. Animals and Their Young; I. incorrect order

## Week 32, Day 4 (page 144)
A. describes the author's feelings; B. whose; C. in, it; D. Also; E. *in-* (not), *over-* (too much), *tele-* (far), *graph-* (written), *bio-* (life), *centi-* (hundred), *deca-* (ten), *sub-* (under); F. dive; G. It helps the author show more clearly what pieces of information are different in each sentence. H. surrender

## Week 33, Day 1 (page 145)
A. Answers will vary. B. cannot; C. con•tain, en•cour•age, pur•pose; D. on, over, through; E. pottery; F. Jose's eyes bulged out of his head. G. park, The sun was shining through the puffy, white clouds, The grassy field was completely empty, Suddenly, a rumbling came from up above, the gray clouds that had formed. H. dessert; I. Whose

## Week 33, Day 2 (page 146)
A. My grandma is teaching me to speak Italian. B. types of fruit; C. that, which; D. plucky, unafraid, bold; E. Don't make a mountain out of a molehill. F. chased; G. fearful, cowardly; H. It surprises them. It seems to come from outside their own minds. It might not be a pleasant thought. I. *-ful*

## Week 33, Day 3 (page 147)
A. dad, will be; B. impatient; C. M, M, S, S, M, S, S; D–E. Answers will vary. F. cause: The desert gets very little rain. effect: So, it stays dry for most of the year. G. actually; H. The New Puppy's Collar; I. misplaced

## Week 33, Day 4 (page 148)
A. describes the author's feelings; B. I want to go outside to play, so I better finish my homework. C. Examples include piece, peace, wheel, and seize. D. In addition; E. costly, The other bike cost less. F. crawl; G. Too much garbage harms Earth. Cities and towns can help people recycle by putting recycling bins in public places. H. continent

## Week 34, Day 1 (page 149)
A. journey, voyage, atlas, sightsee; B. do not always; C. na•tion•al, na•ture, non•sense; D. down the stairs, near the car, around the corner; E. creaky; F. The horse leaped over the fence. G. I had mixed feelings about it. (I felt uncertain.) However, I usually get butterflies in my stomach when I have to stand up in front of a crowd. (I get very nervous.) As it turns out, it was a piece of cake. (It was very easy.) H. shore; I. correct order

## Week 34, Day 2 (page 150)
A. I wanted to go to the fair, but I had homework. B. furniture; C. who, which; D. little, tiny, slight, small; E. Stop and smell the roses. F. scowled; G. mammoth, huge, great, vast; H. He is completely ignoring you. I. *-ion*

## Week 34, Day 3 (page 151)
A. by, buy; B. misplaced; C. A, P, A, P, A, P, P; D. Answers will vary. E. and, but, or; F. cause: after eating too much; effect: most people feel ill; G. voyage; H. Why Bears Shouldn't Sing; I. incorrect order

## Week 34, Day 4 (page 152)
A. fiction; B. Ostriches are native to Africa and can weigh up to 300 pounds. C. chipmunk, nuts; D. Then; E. truthful. Eden didn't lie, even though she could have. F. whole; G. on the other hand, It means you are looking at the second of two different things. H. examine

# Answer Key

## Week 35, Day 1 (page 153)
A. Answers will vary. B. runway; C. car•ni•val, char•coal, cli•mate; D. She was as quick as a cat. He was jumping like a frog. E. swept; F. My little brother is very naughty. G. (pointing to a treasure chest on his front lawn), (running for the treasure chest), (shaking his head), (**Anil** flings open the treasure chest as **Cody** takes a few steps back.); H. break; I. dad

## Week 35, Day 2 (page 154)
A. My homework was done, so I went to Jamie's house. B. parts of a house; C. The cat that lives across the street is really beautiful. I don't know the neighbors who own the cat. D. jot, take down, write, print; E. A penny saved is a penny earned. F. grasped; G. undertake, shameful, weights; H. does; It shows how popular some other school subjects were. I. -en

## Week 35, Day 3 (page 155)
A. shore, sure; B. rewrite; C. F, L, L, L, F, F, L; D. Answers will vary. E. Answers will vary. F. cause: after running; effect: People can find that their legs are sore and weak. G. demand; H. Millie, the Great Messenger Dog; I. incorrect order

## Week 35, Day 4 (page 156)
A. it has stage directions; B. Shirley dislikes social studies, yet she always does well on the tests. C. weigh; D. because; E. movement, LaToya saw something move in the trees. F. wrinkle; G. problem/solution; H. telescope

## Week 36, Day 1 (page 157)
A. ...Answers will vary. B. present; C. un•der•stand, un•hap•py; um•brel•la; D. fish out of water, see eye to eye, draw a blank; E. stiff; F. The water was only two feet deep. G. chimpanze (chimpanzee), crocadile (crocodile), experament (experiment), nayborhood (neighborhood); H. piece; I. isn't

## Week 36, Day 2 (page 158)
A. I do not like peas, nor do I like carrots. B. types of trees; C. The researchers went to sea to record whale songs last Tuesday. D. naughty, wicked, mean; E. Hold your horses! F. persuaded; G. caring, warm, kind; H. stopping yourself from saying something; I. -able

## Week 36, Day 3 (page 159)
A. over, through; B. unusual; C. C, C, I, C, I, C, C; D–E. Answers will vary. F. cause: The Amazon rain forest is being cut down. effect: So, people are trying to stop it. G. willow; H. The Two Ponies' Wild Adventure; I. correct order

## Week 36, Day 4 (page 160)
A. it rhymes; B. After you pass the museum, turn right onto the 12th Street Bridge. C. complete, teacher; D. Because; E. coax, convince, or talk into doing, Garrett offers to do chores to get his mother to agree to let him camp out in Ramon's yard. F. toward; G. The author wants you to feel admiration for Franklin's many accomplishments. H. crocodile

## Week 37, Day 1 (page 161)
A. Atlantic, Arctic, Indian, Pacific; B. past; C. cob•bler; col•lect, com•mand; D. The glass looked like diamonds. The cake was shaped like a football. E. carriage; F. The car screeched to a halt. G. to, two, piece, great, week, There, ponds, eyesight, style; H. ant; I. complete sentence

## Week 37, Day 2 (page 162)
A. "Will you play checkers or fly my kite?" Jen asked. B. family members; C. who; D. reply, statement, answer; E. Better safe than sorry. F. coaxed; G. question, silence, problem; H. I am so good at something that I can do it without thinking or paying attention. I. -ness

## Week 37, Day 3 (page 163)
A. whose, whom; B. discovery; C. F, S, F, S, F, S, F; D. Answers will vary. E. Answers will vary. F. effect: to become a doctor; cause: You have to go to college. G. modern; H. Dr. Howell Helps Hanover; I. incorrect order

## Week 37, Day 4 (page 164)
A. persuade the reader; B. I love spending time with my cousins, but I hardly ever get to see them. C. disguise, surprise; D. Finally; E. No noise, complete quiet; Guillermo didn't hear a sound. F. worried; G. paintings that look like real life and paintings that do not; H. hesitate

## Week 38, Day 1 (page 165)
A. Answers will vary. B. future; C. en•gi•neer, en•dur•ance, ex•per•i•ence; D. I will help Mrs. Ling. She lives on Reed Street. E. painful; F. The cows grazed in the green pasture. G. Answers will vary. H. carrot; I. prefix

## Week 38, Day 2 (page 166)
A. "My soccer game made me late," Matt explained. B. parts of a tree; C. into, at, to, from, by, to; D. allow, understand, agree; E. Cat got your tongue? F. invented; G. argue, deny, refuse, disagree; H. Check students' answers. I. -ning, -ping, -ging

# Answer Key

**Week 38, Day 3 (page 167)**
A. since, where; B. disgrace; C. S, S, R, R, S, S, R; D. Answers will vary. E. Answers will vary. F. cause: It is cold in Colorado. effect: so it gets a lot of snow in winter, G. scenery; H. We're Going to the Mountains; I. correct order

**Week 38, Day 4 (page 168)**
A. tells about an imaginary event; B. Jenna was excited to have a window seat near the airplane's wing. C. today's, rephrase; D. while; E. To achieve what you wanted. Raj believes he will win the spelling bee. F. action; G. Answers will vary. H. instruments

**Week 39, Day 1 (page 169)**
A. Answers will vary. B. two; C. a person's name written by himself or herself; D. disappointment, explanation; E. realize; F. Anuja scaled the tree's crooked branches. G. I have a book report due on Friday. I really need to get started on it. I read the book, but I just never got around to writing the report. If I don't go to Ming's house after school, I can work on it. Next time, I'll definitely start my report earlier. I promised myself I'll never let this happen again. H. hole; I. idiom

**Week 39, Day 2 (page 170)**
A. John said , "Is Charlotte coming on Saturday?" B. sports; C. that, which; D. try, explore, test; E. Time flies when you're having fun. F. burrowed; G. after, beneath, in; H. The Carter family moved into their new apartment. Mrs. Rodriguez drove across the state of Wyoming. I. -est

**Week 39, Day 3 (page 171)**
A. him, into him; B. uneasy; C. S, S, F, F, S, F, S; D–E. Answers will vary. F. cause: when a baby starts to cry; effect: It can be helpful to sing a lullaby. G. cooked; H. The Mysterious Mrs. Mills; I. correct order

**Week 39, Day 4 (page 172)**
A. nonfiction; B. I will be going to the beach this weekend, and I will also be going to the lake. C. Change "will" to "would." D. In the meantime; E. to keep, save, or protect; Kamal is trying to keep the image of the ticket safe forever. F. purpose; G. chronology; H. refrigerator

**Week 40, Day 1 (page 173)**
A. Answers will vary. B. There; C. sends written messages over long distances; D. electricity, immediately, persuade; E. rare; F. The pony nibbled on a clump of grass. G. As we were walking to the park, Neela shouted, "I don't have my glove!" "Where did you leave it?" I asked. "At home, I guess." She was shaking her head, but she was smiling. H. bear; I. prefix

**Week 40, Day 2 (page 174)**
A. "On Labor Day, I visited my grandma," Beth said. B. musical instruments; C. that, whose; D. acted, finished, completed; E. Strike while the iron is hot. F. jammed; G. incomplete, rested, unfinished; H. Across: simile, un-, -ist, onto. Down: inn, must, into. I. -ful

**Week 40, Day 3 (page 175)**
A. Can, must; B. reappeared; C. C, I, C, C, I, C, I; D. Answers will vary. E. Answers will vary. F. effect: Some trees lose their leaves. cause: when autumn comes; G. furnace; H. Are Bees and Wasps the Same?; I. correct order

**Week 40, Day 4 (page 176)**
A. Both have dialogue. B. The year had come to an end, and we were all ready for a break. C. Amy, away, vacation; D. For instance; E. to eat very quickly, Billy eats his food very quickly because he is hungry. F. precious; G. Plants that do not grow in deserts cannot store as much water inside their stems as cactuses can. H. immediately